The celebration of the Bicentennial has been eventful. Our past has been documented by pageants, festivals, films, the work of our writers, photographers, artists, and by this book.

We have appreciated our neighborhoods as they have come together, representing their diversity, their histories, the stories they have to tell, which woven together are the City we have celebrated.

Columbia has faced adversity. Sometimes our economic opportunities have not been as great as others, yet, against a sometimes steeper climb, we have made progress. We have acknowledged our recent history, the spirit of openness and fair play, the sense of community that can be part of the experience of each citizen of the City.

The talents, time and energy of the Bicentennial Committee have made our year-long celebration a reality. Our citizens have been eager to participate, to pay recognition, not only to our history, but to the cause of understanding what Columbia can be. For this we each can be thankful.

Kirkman Finlay, Jr.
Mayor, 1978-1986

T. Patton Adams, Mayor

T. Patton Adams	Rudolph C. Barnes, Jr.	Luther J. Battiste III	Paul Z. Bennett
Luther J. Battiste III	Paul Z. Bennett	E. W. Cromartie II	Francenia B. Heizer
E. W. Cromartie II	William C. Outzs	William C. Outzs	Jim D. N. Papadea

COLUMBIA
Portrait of a City

By
Walter B. Edgar
and
Deborah K. Woolley

Design by
Paula Hennigan Phillips

THE
DONNING COMPANY
PUBLISHERS

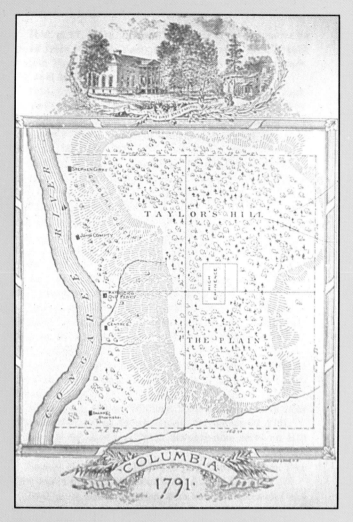

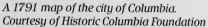

A 1791 map of the city of Columbia.
Courtesy of Historic Columbia Foundation

The Robert Mills House, which has been
restored, was designed by Mills in 1823.
Courtesy of Historic Columbia Foundation

The Columbia cottage was designed to
take advantage of the local climate.
Courtesy of Historic Columbia Foundation

Copyright© 1986 by Walter B. Edgar and Deborah K. Woolley

All rights reserved, including the right to reproduce this work in any form
whatsoever without permission in writing from the publisher, except for brief
passages in connection with a review. For information, write:

The Donning Company/Publishers
5659 Virginia Beach Boulevard
Norfolk, Virginia 23502

Edited by Susan A. Lendvay

Library of Congress Cataloging-in-Publication Data

Edgar, Walter B., 1943-
    Columbia, portrait of a city.
    Bibliography: p.
    Includes index.
    1. Columbia (S.C.)—History—Pictorial works. 2. Columbia (S.C.)—Descrip-
tion—Views. I. Woolley, Deborah K. (Deborah Kohler), 1948-   . II. Title.
F279.C7E34   1986   975.7′71   86-19838
ISBN 0-89865-495-5

Printed in the United States of America

Contents

Columbia was planned as the state's capital, and its future and the state's are closely linked. Photograph by Edward L. Kalsch

The St. Patrick's Day festival in Five Points has become a Columbia tradition. Photograph by Donald K. Woolley

Riverbanks Zoo is recognized as one of the ten best in the nation. Courtesy of Greater Columbia Chamber of Commerce

The annual Mayfest Festival brings thousands of people to the Capitol grounds. Courtesy of Greater Columbia Chamber of Commerce

Talented artists celebrating the city's two hundredth birthday in dance on the State House steps. Photograph by Edward L. Kalsch

Fort Jackson soldiers fire a 75mm-Howitzer salute. Courtesy of U.S. Army

*Children listen to a local storyteller at one
of the city's neighborhood Bicentennial
festivals. Photograph by Edward L. Kalsch*

Foreword

When I first was asked to write this foreword, my thoughts immediately went back fifty years to the Sesquicentennial Celebration and its guiding spirit, James H. Hammond. For years Senator Hammond and I had adjoining offices in the 1200 block of Washington Street. Late in the afternoon we frequently met in the parking lot out back and talked about our city and its growth. On January 21, 1970, the last evening he was alive, he and I stopped for a brief chat beneath a darkening winter sky. And, we talked about the upcoming South Carolina Tricentennial Celebration and Columbia's role in it.

Jim Hammond's life-long devotion to Columbia is not atypical. There have been many others over the course of two centuries who have given of themselves unselfishly to help make South Carolina's capital city a better place than they found it. Expanding city limits and skyscrapers are indicative of progress, but it is people who have given the city its vitality.

This Bicentennial book is a panorama in text, paintings, drawings, and photographs of the two hundred years of Columbia's history. It is appropriate that a number of the photographs come from the archives of Security Federal, the savings and loan association founded by Jim Hammond. The other rare illustrations that appear in this book have been preserved because many other Columbians shared his love for the history of their city.

I have lived in Columbia for seventy years. Today, I'm a rarity, a native Columbian. Being a minority native in a sea of newcomers doesn't really bother me because I know our history. Over the centuries, many thousands have chosen to make their homes in this place. They are welcome. The richness and diversity that is Columbia today are the result of the blend of old and new—people as well as ideas.

As you browse through this book, you'll see that in 1786 Columbia's greatest asset was its people. That is just as true in 1986.

Augustus T. Graydon

The city's Bicentennial parade was a project of area high schools. Photograph by Edward L. Kalsch

Local people enjoy outdoor concerts throughout the city. Courtesy of Greater Columbia Chamber of Commerce

The Bicentennial evening featured Columbia's history portrayed in song and dance. Photograph by Edward L. Kalsch

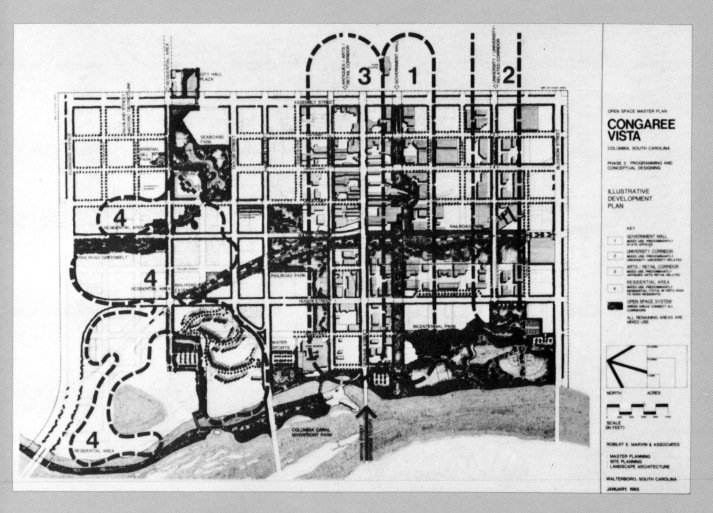

Acknowledgments

This book, like most everything else about Columbia, was the result of planning and cooperation. Many Columbians and Columbia institutions have shared their thoughts and photographs with us. Not all have been used, but each one helped us to piece together the story of South Carolina's capital city. We gratefully acknowledge the assistance of: Mrs. J. O. Butler, the City of Columbia, Columbia Newspapers Inc., Dixie Electronics Inc., Elizabeth Dozier, Fort Jackson Museum, Mrs. William N. Geiger, Augustus T. Graydon, Historic Columbia Foundation, Edward L. Kalsch, McKissick Museums, John Roberson, Security Federal Savings and Loan Association, South Carolina Electric & Gas Company, South Caroliniana Library, USC Information Services, Allen H. Stokes, Victor Tutte, Candy Waites, and Don Woolley.

A special thank you to our families: Amelia, Betty, and Eliza Edgar and Don Woolley. Without this support and understanding, it would not have been possible to complete this project on time.

Walter B. Edgar   Deborah K. Woolley

COLUMBIA
portrait of a city

"Columbia, founded within these twenty years, is the seat of government for the state of South Carolina. It is built about two hundred fathoms from the . . . River, upon an uniform spot of ground. The number of its houses does not exceed two hundred; they are almost all built of wood, and painted grey and yellow; and although there are few of them more than two stories high, they have a very respectable appearance."

Andre Michaux
Travels to the Westward
Alleghany Mountains (1805)

ONE

GROWING UP
1786-1860

The development of the city of Columbia had its origins in the quarter century that preceded the American Revolution. During the 1750s and 1760s, tens of thousands of Scots-Irish and Germans from Pennsylvania and English from Virginia moved into the South Carolina piedmont—or the "backcountry," as it was called. This massive influx of new settlers led to social and political instability in the backcountry and constant friction with the older coastal region, the "lowcountry."

By the time of the American Revolution, there were nearly twice as many potential voters in the backcountry as in the lowcountry. The successful war for American independence led backcountry leaders to demand participation in a government that their blood had helped establish. The lowcountry elite who dominated South Carolina state government had no intention of letting the backcountry settlers have any real say in state affairs.

In an attempt to assuage the backcountry, the General Assembly voted to move the state capital from Charleston to a piece of land belonging to Col. Thomas Taylor along the banks of the Congaree near the confluence of the

Broad and Saluda rivers. During the course of the debate, Sen. Arnoldus VanderHorst of Charleston snidely suggested that the new capital in the wilderness be called the "Town of Refuge" because it was beyond the pale of the law. To this, Sen. John Lewis Gervais of Saxe Gothe (Lexington) County replied that he hoped that the oppressed of every land might find refuge under the wings of Columbia. Gervais's retort struck a responsive chord among his fellow legislators, and, after a close vote, they chose Columbia rather than Washington as the name for the new capital city.

On March 22, 1786, the General Assembly passed the legislation necessary to create the new capital. By September, lots were being sold in Charleston, but the town would not be laid out until 1787.

Columbia was a planned city from the beginning. John Gabriel Guignard surveyed a square, two miles on each side, and laid out streets in a regular grid plan. Senate and Assembly streets, named for the legislature, were to be grand boulevards and the main arteries. All streets running parallel to the river and Assembly were named for Revolutionary War generals and heroes. Those

The Col. Thomas Taylor mansion sat on the present Arsenal Hill. A painting depicts the plantation around 1790. Courtesy of South Caroliniana Library

east of Assembly were named after officers of the Continental line. West of Assembly, the streets bore the names of South Carolina's patriots who had helped the state win its independence. The streets perpendicular to the river were named for just about anything—their geographical location, the first President and his lady, local personages, and South Carolina agricultural products. The naming of the streets after state figures and crops underscored the fact that Columbia was a capital city for all South Carolinians, and not just a select few, as had been its predecessor.

In 1788, work began on the new State House designed by James Hoban, a young Irish-born architect from Charleston. By January 1790, state records had been moved to Columbia, and the General Assembly met in the new building for the first time. Later that spring, a constitutional convention met in the State House and Columbia was made the permanent state capital—but not without a bitter last-ditch effort by some lowcountry citizens to return it to Charleston. No doubt, these gentlemen were unhappy that the little frontier town provided "no sermons, balls or oyster pies" with which they could amuse themselves. Columbia stayed a frontier town for a few years, but then Rome wasn't built in a day and neither was Charleston.

In May 1791, when President George Washington made his famous tour of the southern states, he visited Columbia. He stayed in town for three days and was entertained by the local gentry at a dinner in the State House. The first President described Columbia as "laid out upon a large scale, but. . . is now an uncleared wood with very few houses in it. . . ."

Washington, however, was impressed with the State House, and it is believed that he invited its architect to come north to help design the new federal capital city. Whether or not an invitation was given at that time, Hoban did enter the design competition for the President's house and won. The White House in Washington, D.C., is a carbon copy of South Carolina's first State House in Columbia. This would not be the last time that an architectural idea was used first in South Carolina's new capital and later in the nation's capital.

The "uncleared wood" was gradually pushed back in the last decade of the 18th century. By 1790, a regular stage line was established linking Charleston and Columbia. The town's first newspaper, the *Columbia Gazette*, appeared in 1791. Although it lasted only one year, it was followed by others so that Columbia always had a newspaper of its own.

The establishing of churches is an indication of the taming of the frontier. The first one was organized by the Presbyterians, who called it appropriately, First Church. In a letter to a young clergyman, Col. Thomas Taylor and Benjamin Waring, two of Columbia's founding fathers, pled with him to accept their call "as it is greatly contrary to the interests of a young town to be growing up without the Sabbath day's observation." In regular succession, other denominations organized: Washington Street Methodist (1803); First Baptist

(1807); Trinity Episcopal (1812); Hebrew Benevolent Society (1822); St. Peter's Roman Catholic (1824); and Ebenezer Lutheran (1828).

Like many other structures in Columbia, the churches reflected the frontier character of the place. Washington Street Methodist's first building was described as a "very neat, pretty building," but inside the walls were "not plaistered—and the seats are merely movable benches. . . ." The first Trinity Episcopal Church was a simple wooden building at the intersection of Sumter and Gervais streets. Well into the first quarter of the nineteenth century, visitors commented on the large number of wooden buildings, many which appeared to have been hastily constructed.

Appearances, however, can be deceiving. Columbians were striving to make the town more than just a place where a few state offices were located and where the General Assembly met for several weeks every December. The Columbia Academy [for males] opened its doors in 1797; twenty years later, its female counterpart began operation.

The first sort of "self-rule" was established in 1798 when the General Assembly passed an act creating a seven-man commission—elected annually by the town's voters—to oversee the city's markets and streets and to suppress gambling. Real self-government did not come until December 19, 1805, when the legislature, in response to a petition from the local citizenry, voted to incorporate the town of Columbia. The act called for annual election of an intendant (mayor) and six wardens (councilmen). In 1806, John Taylor was elected Columbia's first intendant. Columbia already had been made the seat of Richland County in 1799. These actions by the legislature greatly aided the little settlement's development as did the chartering of the South Carolina College in 1801.

The creation of the college was yet another attempt by lowcountry citizens to stave off genuine political reform and legislative reapportionment. In proposing the college, Gov. John Drayton expressed the hope that "the friendships of young men would thence be promoted and strengthened throughout the State, and our political union much advanced thereby." The college's proponents intended that it become the training ground for the state's ruling elite.

The college accepted its first students in 1805 and within two decades achieved the goal of its founders. Located on what was then the southern edge of town, the college's brick buildings made quite an impression on visitors.

The college and its activities played a major role in Columbia throughout the antebellum years. Commencement was in December, and so was the annual legislative session. The commencement festivities included academic processions, student debates, and a grand ball. In a time when a sharp wit and quick tongue were much admired, legislators watched the debates with keen interest. Many a young man's political future was assured by his performance in the oratorical contests.

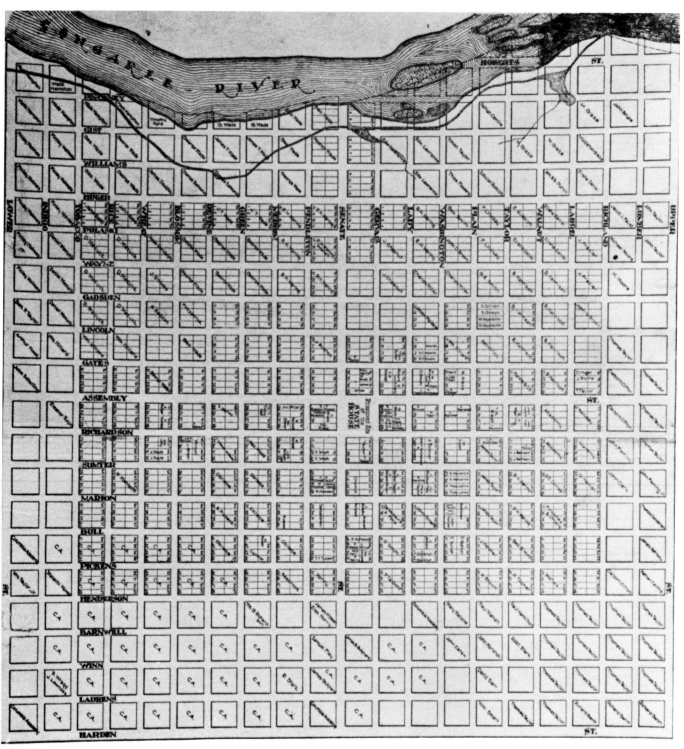

A map of Columbia, a planned city, in
1786. The original street names show on
the map as well as the original purchasers
of the property. The first sale of property
was recorded September 26, 1786, and
the map was used to record property sales
until around 1806 when the town was
incorporated. Courtesy of South Caroliniana Library

Actions of the General Assembly aside, it was the cotton gin that did as much as anything to help transform Columbia from a dusty little frontier community into a bustling interior market town. The planting of upland or short staple cotton reached Richland County before 1800. By 1806, there were two gin manufacturers in town supplying the needs of South Carolina's expanding cotton kingdom.

In 1820, South Carolina was the leading cotton-producing state in the nation and Columbia cotton factors handled tens of thousands of bales a year. Business that once had gone to Charleston now came to Columbia. Transportation of the bulky cotton bales was made easier by steamships that traveled inland via the Santee and Congaree rivers.

Intent on tapping the cotton markets further inland, Columbians began pushing for the development of the Columbia Canal to bypass the rapids just above the city. Soon, Columbians joined with other investors in forming the South Carolina Canal and Railroad Company.

When George Washington's old comrade-in-arms, the Marquis de Lafayette, paid a visit in March 1825, he found much more than an "uncleared wood with very few houses." The little frontier town was growing up. Some 500 houses, "many of them handsome," were scattered throughout the city. Of particular note were the homes of Ainsley Hall and Wade Hampton on Walnut (Blanding) Street. The Asylum (State Hospital), designed by Robert Mills, incorporated the latest and most advanced features for the humane treatment of the mentally ill.

Col. Abram Blanding's waterworks were a marvel. A steam engine forced water up 120 feet from springs near the river bank into cast iron pipes running beneath much of the downtown area. Individual families could tap into the system if they chose. Despite the availability of this modern convenience, many opted for individual wells until after the Civil War.

A bridge across the Congaree was under construction in 1825. It replaced several earlier ones that had been washed away by floods. The two-lane covered wooden bridge would be 1,350 feet long, resting on fourteen solid granite piers.

By 1830, the bridge had been completed and so had the Jonathan Maxcy Monument on the South Carolina College campus. Erected in honor of the school's first president, the granite and marble monument is indicative of Robert Mills's fascination with the Egyptian obelisk. Later, when he moved from Columbia to Washington, D.C., his "Egyptian phase" found full expression in the Washington Monument.

As the decade of the 1820s ended, Columbians celebrated the inauguration of native South Carolinian Andrew Jackson as President of the United States with fireworks and cannon salutes. Unfortunately, South Carolina's joy in Jackson's election would soon turn to dismay with the Nullification Crisis of 1832-1833.

A number of issues surfaced that made South Carolina's political leadership unhappy in the early 1830s. Northern support for the Tariff of 1828 and the new abolition movement seemed to threaten the state's economic foundations. A majority of Columbians opposed nullification, but during November 1832, the town was the site of the Nullification Convention. Eventually a compromise was reached with the federal government, but many saw this event simply as a prelude to civil war.

Colonel Thomas Taylor's plantation was on the site selected for Columbia. Taylor, who became one of the first commissioners of the new town, was given the right to reserve two acres provided he did not build on it in a way inconsistent with the city's plan. Courtesy of South Caroliniana Library

The political ferment of the 1830s gave rise to a number of newspapers including *Southern Times* and *The South Carolinian*. From 1832 until 1860, Columbians had a choice of at least two newspapers, and usually three.

As Columbia grew, the South Carolina College grew. Under the presidency of Robert W. Barnwell (1835-1841) began an ambitious building program. Two new dormitories, a faculty residence, and the first separate college library building in the country were erected. The campus was surrounded by a six-foot-high brick wall to isolate students from the town.

Improvements on the campus were mirrored by activity all over town. The town fathers purchased Colonel Blanding's waterworks for $50,000 so this essential service would be truly a municipal enterprise. In 1838, contracts were let to complete the railroad from Branchville to Columbia, thus linking the capital with the port city of Charleston. Four years later, on June 28, 1842, the first train arrived in Columbia. That same year the General Assembly established the Arsenal Academy to provide military training for young South Carolinians.

Columbians were very military-oriented in the decades preceding the Civil War. By law, all white males between eighteen and fifty had to belong to a militia unit. There were seven uniformed companies in the capital city, and they paraded regularly. The Fourth of July always was celebrated by the companies in a combined parade.

Besides the militia, all white males between eighteen and sixty had to help patrol the streets (in lieu of a regular police force) unless they belonged to one of the volunteer fire companies. The primary purpose of the patrol was to control the black population and thwart any hint of slave insurrection. Although the black population of the city was 50.8 percent in 1840, Richland County's population was 67.5 percent black. In a state where blacks were a decided majority of the population, there was a real concern over the possibility of a slave rebellion.

Every evening, a curfew bell rang, and blacks were supposed to be off the streets unless they had a pass. From May to September the bell rang at 10:00 P.M., and the remainder of the year, at 9:00 P.M.

There were free blacks in Columbia (149 in 1840; 250 in 1860), but, by law, they had only limited freedom. One of the centers of the free black community was the home of Cecilia Mann and William Simons on the northeast corner of Richland and Marion streets. In this house, the First Calvary Baptist Church and a number of black civic and social organizations were formed.

In 1841, the Vigilant Fire Company, comprised of black Columbians, joined with the town's only white company, the Independent, to control Columbia's first major conflagration. Almost a city block along Richardson (Main) Street between Plain (Hampton) and Taylor streets was destroyed. The "Brick Range," two two-story masonry buildings containing the principal stores in town were lost, as were the printing offices of the *South Carolinian*.

The fire of 1841 did little to hinder Columbia's growth in the 1840s or 1850s. In 1844, business leaders formed the Columbia Commercial Association, a forerunner of the Chamber of Commerce, to promote the town's development.

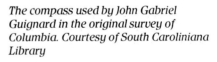

The compass used by John Gabriel Guignard in the original survey of Columbia. Courtesy of South Caroliniana Library

Their endeavors met with considerable success.

Columbia received a new charter in 1854 as a city with a mayor and six aldermen—two from each of the city's wards—elected annually. Railroads were completed in 1852 to link Columbia with Charlotte and Greenville. That same year, gas lightning was introduced. By 1860 it had become commonplace. The first State Fair in 1856, held at the old fairgrounds off Elmwood Avenue, was a resounding success. The last remains of the frontier town began to disappear when the various churches replaced their original wooden structures with larger masonry ones.

In 1847, Trinity Episcopal Church completed its new Gothic-style edifice opposite the State House. Trinity's stucco exterior, tinted and scored in imitation of brownstone, was an indication of popular tastes. The brick building on the South Carolina College campus soon received similar treatment. When the new First Presbyterian (1854) and First Baptist (1859) churches were completed, their exteriors bore the brownstone look. Throughout the city, foundations and chimneys were modernized or built in the new fashion.

Private residences frequently took the form of raised Greek Revival cottages. So prevalent was this building type that it was known in South Carolina as a "Columbia Cottage." In Columbia's climate, the raised cottage with its enclosed basement was a practical dwelling. Halls running from the front to back of the house, windows that went to the floor and fourteen or fifteen-foot ceilings, all were designed to help mitigate the effects of the semi-tropical summer heat. More than one visitor compared a July or August visit in Columbia with a trip to India. The Indian comparison might have been brought to mind not only by the heat but also by the Pride of India (chinaberry) trees which lined the town's streets.

The local temperature may have been made hotter by the political climate. Between 1850 and 1860, South Carolina's leaders were looking for an opportune moment to leave the union. While some Columbians such as Wade Hampton III and William Campbell Preston cautioned against outright secession, the mood of the citzenry seemed to be with the radical secessionist camp.

In April 1860, the state Democratic Convention met in Columbia, and the radicals, as the outright secessionists were called, carried the day. Their actions—with those of like-minded Southerners meeting at the national Democratic Convention in Charleston in May—led to the disruption of the party and the foregone conclusion that the Republicans would win the presidential election in November.

When Keziah Goodwyn Hopkins Brevard of Lower Richland County heard the news she wrote in her diary: "Oh my God! This morning heard that Lincoln was elected—I had prayed that God would thwart this election in some way and I have prayed for my country. Lord we know not what is to be the result of this...."

The results were as swift and as certain as Lincoln's election had been. The South Carolina General Assembly called for a special convention of the people to determine the state's future in the Union. The Secession Convention opened in Columbia on December 17, 1860, at the First Baptist Church. The city was thronged with politicians and visitors—one of whom was most unwelcomed: as delegates to the convention were arriving, smallpox broke out. There were not that many cases, but the convention voted to adjourn to Charleston. There, on December 20, 1860, South Carolina voted unanimously to leave the union it had helped form.

"The Union is Dissolved" emblazoned the headlines in extra editions of the state's newspapers. In Columbia, the news was greeted with pealing bells, bonfires and militia company parades. In almost a party mood, South Carolina rushed out of the Union and into war—a war which began at Fort Sumter in Charleston.

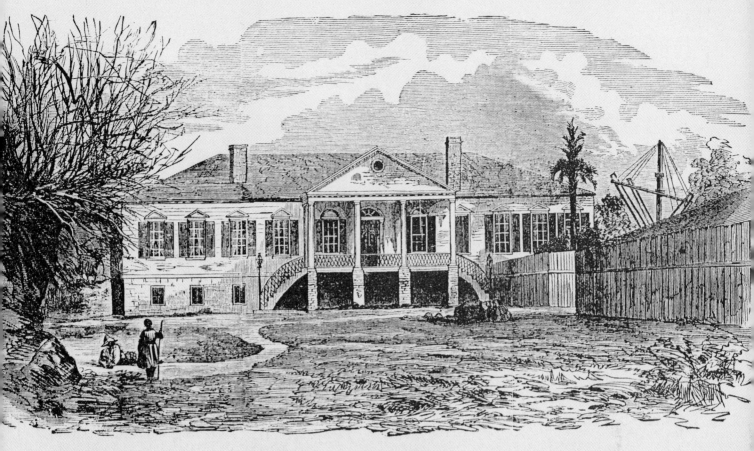

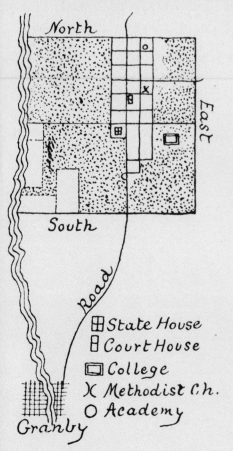

North

East

South

Road

Granby

⊞ State House
⊟ Court House
▭ College
✗ Methodist Ch.
○ Academy

A drawing shows the first State House in Columbia in the early 1800s. Courtesy of South Caroliniana Library

An 1805 sketch of the first plot of Columbia was found in the diary of Edward Hooker, an early visitor to the newly formed city. Courtesy of South Caroliniana Library

Fisher's Mill on Rocky Branch was one of several mills that operated in the Columbia area in the 1800s. Courtesy of South Caroliniana Library

The third bridge to cross the Congaree River at Columbia was a wooden structure on stone pilings. It was the first one that survived for any period of time. Courtesy of South Caroliniana Library

The South Carolina Female Collegiate Institute at Barhamville, on the northeast edge of the city, opened in 1829 to offer area women a higher education. The painting depicts the school in the mid-1830s. Courtesy of South Caroliniana Library

The Saluda Factory, a cotton mill built in the early 1800s, had one thousand employees by 1862 when it was supplying the Confederate government. Burned by General Sherman in 1865, it was located on the west bank of the Saluda across from the present-day Riverbanks Zoo. Courtesy of South Caroliniana Library

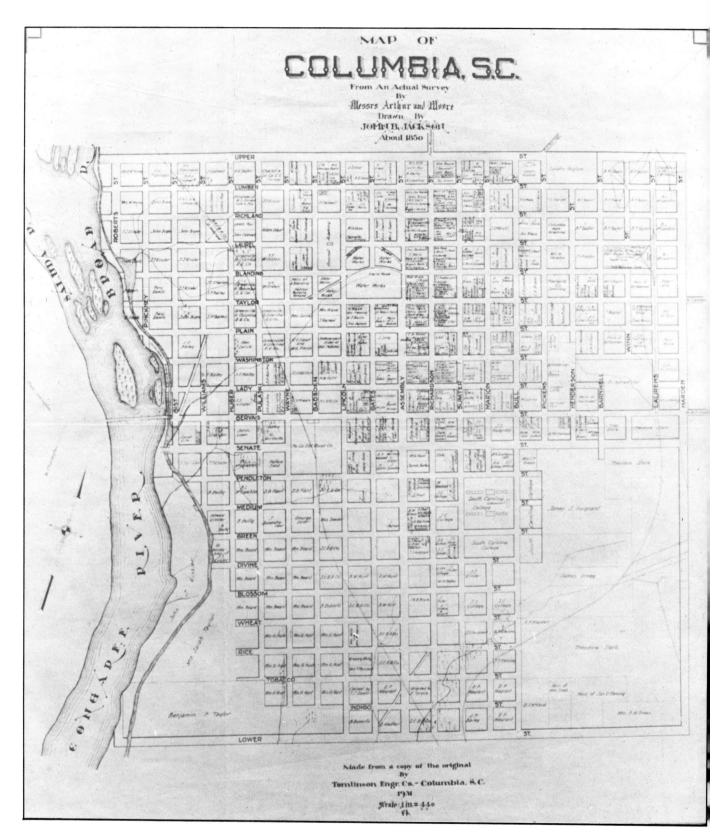

A map from a survey by Messrs. Arthur and Moore show Columbia's growth by 1850. Courtesy of South Caroliniana Library

An artist's view, painted around 1859, of Columbia in the future with its planned new State House standing next to the original at the far right. Designed by John R. Niernsee in 1854, it looked different when it was finally completed early in the twentieth century. Courtesy of South Caroliniana Library

Lower Richland County was home to several major plantations. Kensington Plantation, on the banks of the Wateree River, was a unique one—both in house design and operations. Courtesy of Historic Columbia Foundation

23

A painting of South Carolina College Horseshoe around 1850. Courtesy of South Caroliniana Library

The Columbia Female Academy, which first appeared in public records in 1815, was at Washington and Marion streets. In 1824, the school had 110 students, 45 being boarders. Tuition and board was $175 to $200 a year. Courtesy of Historic Columbia Foundation

The Robert Mills building at the State Hospital, originally the Lunatic Asylum, was completed in 1828. Designed by Mills, it was innovative in design and unique in the facilities provided for humane treatment of the mentally ill. The building still stands today, but the design was altered as additional phases were built. Courtesy of Historic Columbia Foundation

People have long puzzled over the actual date of this photograph. The Commercial Bank operated in Columbia from 1831 until the city burned in 1865. Most histories report that all businesses on Main Street burned, and there are no reports of the establishment of another Commercial Bank in Columbia after the war. The street light apparently is gas, so the picture could have been taken between 1852, when the city first installed gaslights, and 1865. Courtesy of Security Federal Savings and Loan Association

An early city jail in Columbia. Courtesy of South Caroliniana Library

This photograph of an antebellum church is thought by some to be Christ Episcopal Church, but historians at the University of South Carolina believe it probably is the original St. Peters Roman Catholic Church. Courtesy of Security Federal Savings and Loan Association

27

"Columbia will have bitter cause to remember the visit of Sherman's army. Even if peace and prosperity soon return to the land, not in this generation nor the next—no, not even for a century—can this city or the state recover. . . . The ancient homesteads where have gathered sacred associations, the heritages of many generations, are swept away."

George Ward Nichols
The Story of the Great March from the Diary of a Staff Officer (1865)

TWO
WAR AND
RECONSTRUCTION
1860-1877

I n 1860, Columbia was a fair-sized town with a population of 8,000. Visitors commented on what a "handsome place" it was. The wide, tree-lined streets, elegant private residences, and impressive public buildings presented a pleasing appearance. Richardson (Main) Street had developed as the town's commercial and economic center. Of the more than two hundred business and professional entries in the 1860 city directory, nearly 75 percent were located on the busy artery that ran north from the capitol building on Gervais Street toward the city limits. This concentration of commercial activity was convenient for business, but it would prove nearly fatal in 1865.

Almost any service or product could be found that a Columbian or visitor might desire. There were four major hotels and eleven boarding houses for out-of-town guests. The best-known were the Congaree and the United States hotels—both located at the intersection of Richardson and Lady streets. Small shops lined both sides of Richardson Street: from bakers, booksellers and clothiers to florists, grocers, and upholsterers.

Noticeably absent in 1860 were any major manufacturing operations. There were two breweries, three carriage manufacturers, two planing mills and two iron foundries outside the town; Dr. Robert W. Gibbes's Saluda Factory was one of only a handful of textile mills in South Carolina. Lawyers (thirteen) outnumbered churches (ten).

The most prominent landmark in town was the new State House. The cornerstone had been laid in 1851, and construction had been going on for nearly a decade. When Secession came, work ceased and most of the European stonecutters and masons left. While some of the State House workmen left of their own accord, others were forced to flee because of their political opinions.

In the weeks following the Secession Convention, there were rumors of slave insurrections. One was supposed to occur during Christmas 1860. As a precaution, all members of the city's military companies were ordered to take their weapons home and were issued ammunition. There was, however, no attempted insurrection as the rumors proved to be part of the excitement that gripped the city and state.

Even dissent was not tolerated—P. F. Frazee, a carriage manufacturer, was whipped, tarred, and feathered and

The Columbia Male Academy, founded in 1792, was on the block bounded by Laurel, Richland, Pickens, and Henderson streets when this picture of the cadets in Confederate uniforms was taken in the 1860s. The school became Taylor School in 1905 and closed in 1964. Courtesy of Security Federal Savings and Loan Association

"sent away to the North" because of his abolitionist views.

Another result of the excitement of the times was the mobilization of the militia companies. The College Cadet Company, acting on its own initiative, defied the faculty and went to Charleston. Other local units also went to the coast and, in April 1861, participated in the first battle of the war.

Because of its location, Columbia became the major mobilization center for the upper part of the state. Initially, the old fairgrounds were used, but later a training camp was established at Lightwood Knot Springs, near Killian, about ten miles from town.

The Confederate government operated Camp Lightwood Knot Springs and a number of other facilities in the capital city. Camp Sorghum, a prisoner-of-war camp, was located on the Congaree River, and a holding area for "Galvanized Yankees"—prisoners who had taken an oath of allegiance to the Confederacy—was established on the outskirts of town. Many Confederate agencies made Columbia their state headquarters, including the Bureau of Conscription and the medical, commissary, quartermaster, and paymaster departments.

Very early in the war, the city became a major center for the Confederate war effort. In 1862, official Confederate printing operations were moved from Richmond, Virginia, to Columbia. Widows and wives of Confederate soldiers were employed in producing the South's currency and bonds. A military hospital was established at the old fairgrounds, but in 1862 it was moved to the South Carolina College campus. After the hospital was moved, Prof. Joseph LeConte established and managed the Confederacy's largest medical manufacturing facility at the fairgrounds. In addition, saltpeter works were opened near the state hospital to make one of the crucial ingredients for gunpowder.

In addition to these government-owned facilities, there were a number of local business enterprises that had contracts to manufacture supplies for the Confederate Army. One thousand workers were employed at the Saluda Factory which produced woolen cloth. In or near the city, factories opened up to make socks, buttons, shoes, uniforms, and hats for the army. Gunpowder was manufactured in a mill built between the banks of the Congaree and the Columbia Canal. The city's foundries turned out bayonets, swords, cannons, bombshells, cannonballs and minié balls. A Confederate armory to store these munitions was located just below the Congaree River Bridge.

The new industries and other war-related activities helped boost the city's population, as did military action along the coast. Within four years, Columbia's population had tripled to approximately 25,000.

During wartime, Columbia was a place of marked contrasts—poverty side by side with prosperity. Inflation, fueled in large measure by the unbacked Confederate currency printed in the city, caused financial distress for many. Most vulnerable were soldiers' wives. One young wife bitterly complained that she was being gouged by war profiteers. Her husband's monthly salary was only eleven dollars, while a cord of wood cost her thirty-four dollars.

In April 1863, the Corn Association was formed to provide some relief. By September, two thousand people were receiving assistance. The Board of Relief in 1864 had more than eleven hundred names on its rolls. One group of women took matters into their own hands—they raided Lyles's Grocery Store on the edge of town and loaded up their wagons with needed provisions. They were stopped by the sheriff who did nothing because of Lyles's mean reputation and the fact that all were either wives or widows of soldiers.

While some segments of society suffered, others lived it up. "Columbia was one of the liveliest places in the Confederacy," with balls, fetes, grand soirees, picnics, concerts, and benefits of all sorts. Many of the entertainments were fund-raisers for the Confederate cause, but all of the merriment in the capital caused considerable ill-will elsewhere in the state.

Although located far from the front, the city's women came face to face with the ugly side of the country's first modern war. The Wayside Hospital and the Ladies' Hospital were created to meet the needs of wounded soldiers being sent south from Virginia. During the course of the war, the Wayside Hospital at the South Carolina Railroad Depot on Gervais Street assisted more than seventy-five thousand servicemen. The condition of the wounded and dying brought the war home in a forceful fashion.

Not only did Columbians assist soldiers passing through their city, they also provided wayside hospitals in Virginia for South Carolina soldiers and headed up a state-wide soldiers' relief association that every month sent railroad cars full of food and clothing to the front.

As the war dragged on, the Conscription Bureau issued calls for all males aged sixteen to sixty. Slaves were drafted to work on coastal fortifications. Among those taken from Richland County was Jacob Stroyer, who belonged to the Singletons of Kensington Plantation. His memoirs, published after the war, provide a rare pre-1865 glimpse into the world of black South Carolinians.

Inflation, the constant parade of wounded, the draft, and the shortages of almost all necessities brought the distant war home to Columbians. There was little they could do about inflation, the casualties, and the draft, but shortages were circumvented with a little bit of imagination and ingenuity.

Clothing was used and reused. Instead of Paris bonnets, Columbia women fashioned hats from palmetto fronds. Sugar, salt, and soap were imported luxuries—locally made soft soap, evaporated sea salt, and sorghum were substitutes. Coffee simply was not available at any price. Instead, parched sweet potatoes, wheat, rye, okra seed, corn, and peanuts were used to produce hot beverages. According to many ac-

Trinity Episcopal was the fourth church to be organized in the city. This picture was taken around 1862. Courtesy of Trinity Cathedral

Sutler Tent, located south of the Robert Mills Building outside the State Asylum, was active throughout the Civil War. Courtesy of South Caroliniana Library

counts, rye was the most popular.

As 1864 ended, Columbians found themselves facing not only severe shortages, but also Gen. William Tecumseh Sherman's Union troops. Law and order was breaking down. There was no gas available for street lights, and the newspapers commented that it was not safe for decent folks to be on the streets after dark. Burglary and theft were common occurrences. No one's pigs and chickens were safe—even in backyard pens. In November, vandals sacked Gen. Wade Hampton's home and scrawled anti-war graffiti on the walls.

When Sherman presented Savannah to President Lincoln as a Christmas present, South Carolinians knew that 1865 would see the Union Army in the Palmetto State. Appeals for assistance went unheeded, as the Confederacy simply lacked the strength. Gen. Wade Hampton was ordered home to help with his state's defenses, but he wasn't given the manpower to do the job.

Where would Sherman strike—Charleston or Columbia? The Confederates divided their forces to protect both cities, but all they could do was perform delaying actions.

Almost as a last hurrah, Columbia's women held a Great Bazaar in mid-January 1865 to raise funds for the cause. The State House was turned into a gala setting for goods from all areas of the Confederacy. The bazaar lasted only two weeks, however, as Sherman's entry into South Carolina on February 1 led to its early closing.

It took only two weeks for the federal forces to reach the banks of the Congaree, and on February 16 they began to shell the city. Several cannonballs hit the partially completed State House, and later generations marked the spots with bronze stars. Retreating Confederates burned all the bridges into Columbia, but Union Army engineers needed only twenty-four hours to throw across a pontoon bridge.

Early the next morning—February 17, 1865—the city awakened to the sound of a tremendous explosion. Looters, plundering the government stores at the South Carolina Railroad Depot, dropped a torch into some gunpowder. Thirty-five thieves met their Maker, and the depot was destroyed. At nine o'clock, General Hampton ordered the withdrawal of his troops and told Mayor Thomas Jefferson Goodwyn to surrender the city.

Goodwyn and three councilmen proceeded out Broad River Road where they met the advancing Union Army. They surrendered the city and were assured that all private property would be protected.

The horrors of the next twenty-four hours would be burned into the memory of all Columbians.

Within hours of their arrival in the capital, the majority of the Union soldiers were drunk. Some citizens, thinking they would somehow placate the Yankees, had refused to destroy the medicinal whiskey belonging to the Confederate government and had given it to the soldiers. It didn't take much

whiskey to turn the army into a drunken mob. After all, the soldiers had been on the march for weeks and had not had a square meal in several days.

About dusk, a fire was reported in a bordello on lower Gervais Street. It was contained, but other fires broke out in different parts of the city. Fanned by high winds, the flames spread rapidly until the central portion of the city was ablaze.

William Gilmore Simms described the city on the morning of the eighteenth: "Great spouts of flame spread aloft in canopies of sulphurous cloud—wreaths of sable, edged with sheet lightnings, wrapped the skies, and, at short intervals, the falling tower and the tottering wall, avalanche-like, went down with thunderous sound, sending up at every crash great billowy showers of glowing fiery embers."

The rising sun the next day revealed the extent of the damage—the entire commercial district on Richardson Street was gone. The fire had done its worst in a thirty-six-square-block area bounded by Assembly, Gervais, Bull and Upper (Elmwood) streets. Not only was the heart of the city's business district wiped out, but so were a number of private dwellings.

The destruction of one home usually put more than one family on the streets. Columbia had become a refugee center, and most residents had given shelter to kinfolk who had fled the advancing army. And most of these refugees were women, children, and the elderly.

Who burned Columbia is a question that has been hotly debated for more than a century. While there are documented instances of Union soldiers torching private homes, there are also accounts of them saving burning buildings. Federal authorities blamed the blaze on retreating Confederates, but Columbians were convinced that General Sherman was responsible.

In all accounts, whether Confederate or Union, there are references to the strong northwesterly winds that gusted in all directions. Until the winds died down about three o'clock on the morning of the eighteenth, the fire could not be controlled.

The controversy probably will never be settled to everyone's satisfaction. No matter what the evidence, Columbians who went through the conflagration were certain that the Yankees had burned their town. Their perceptions of the events would be handed down as part of the community's heritage.

As a modern footnote to the burning controversy, it must be pointed out that Columbians themselves—usually in the name of "progress"—have destroyed more antebellum structures since 1865 than were lost on the night of February 17.

There might be debate about the burning of Columbia, but there can be no question as to who looted it. Not only was the town a refugee center, but many valuables from Georgia and the Carolina coast had been sent here for safekeeping. The city's bank vaults were bulging with church silver, jewelry, stocks, and bonds. Wagonloads of plunder accompanied the Union forces northward.

The army remained in town for a few more days and destroyed any Confederate offices and supplies that had escaped damage on the seventeenth. The departing forces left a few scrawny milk cows which were slaughtered and distributed to the population through relief stations. Appeals for help went out to nearby towns. Supply wagons from all parts of the state, North Carolina, and Georgia brought food, clothing, and medicine for the stricken populace.

After a trek through the upper part of the state, Julian Selby and some fellow newspapermen procured enough printing supplies and equipment to start *The Columbia Phoenix*. On March 21, 1865, the first issue appeared "from the ashes of the city."

Businessmen began to recoup, and by June some twenty-five stores had reopened in temporary quarters, often only wooden shacks hastily thrown together. Scarcity was still the order of the day, as illustrated by the apocryphal tale of the young lad who was seen digging frantically around a groundhog hole. When told by an observer that he couldn't possibly catch the animal, the lad replied, "I've got to have him; the preacher is coming and there's no meat in the house." Hunger was very much a fact of life for all Columbians, black and white.

The imposition of Congressional Reconstruction dramatically altered life in the capital city. In the elections for delegates to the Constitutional Convention of 1868, blacks voted for the first time. Three of the four delegates from Richland County were black. One of them, an ex-slave from Columbia named Beverly Nash, later became a state senator and one of the state's political power brokers during Reconstruction. The constitution adopted by that convention provided for political equality and equal opportunity for all South Carolinians.

Blacks and their political allies controlled the General Assembly and most local offices throughout the state. Corruption was rampant at all levels of government. In that respect, South Carolina was no different from her sister states to the north and south. It was an era that one historian has termed "The Great Barbecue."

In addition to locals who participated in the orgy of spending, outsiders came to the capital seeking their fortunes. Many were venal—intent only on lining their pockets at the expense of the state and of the ex-slaves they ostensibly came South to assist. Not all outsiders fell into this category, however. During Reconstruction, a young Ohio physician named Wheeler came to town and built a sawmill, a fashionable hotel on Main Street, and a home on a hill in the southeastern portion of the city. He remained in Columbia only a few years, but left his name on Wheeler's Hill.

Columbia's experience mirrored that of other towns across the nation. Its bonded indebtedness soared. Future generations were saddled with an $850,000 debt with only about $75,000 in physical improvements to show for it. The largest single item was a new City Hall and Opera House which cost some $300,000. When it accidentally burned in 1899, it was described as a building "conceived in sin and born in iniquity." When Columbians celebrated their Sesquicentennial in 1936, the city debt incurred during Reconstruction was still being paid off.

Columbians not only had to cope with what their own city government was doing, they witnessed firsthand many of the shenanigans in state government. Millions of dollars were misspent, but Main Street merchants benefited, as the state's Reconstruction elite spent lavishly—in cash.

When not dealing with politics, Columbians amused themselves quietly. Old families, many with limited incomes, entertained with homemade cake, lemonade, and a fiddler. They learned to play baseball—a Yankee import. In 1868, an enterprising businessman purchased five wooden velocipedes (bicycles) and operated a rink on Assembly Street. Rides cost ten cents.

There was no legal segregation, but most white Columbians carefully distanced themselves from blacks and vice versa. Blacks withdrew in large numbers from white churches where before 1865 they had worshiped with their masters. All-black congregations, such as Bethel African Methodist Episcopal Church (1866), sprang up in various parts of the city. Benedict College, founded in 1870, provided higher educational opportunities for those black South Carolinians choosing not to attend the fully integrated University of South Carolina.

As taxpayers' bills mounted, the pre-Civil War elite began a campaign to regain control of the state. In the gubernatorial election of 1876, Columbia's hero, Wade Hampton III, was the Democratic Party nominee. The campaigning was furious and violence was widespread—on both sides. The governor disbanded all Democratic Rifle Clubs (heirs to the antebellum militia units), but some maintained their identities in none-too-subtle fashion. The Columbia Flying Artillery called itself the "Hampton and Tilden Musical Club with four twelve-pounder flutes!"

The election was extremely close. Both Hampton and his Republican opponent declared victory. For six months Columbia was an armed camp. Gov. D. H. Chamberlain remained in office only with the support of federal bayonets. When Pres. Rutherford B. Hayes ordered the federal troops out of South Carolina on April 10, 1877, Hampton and his followers claimed the right to govern that they felt they had won in November. The plan imposed by Congress to reorder—and reconstruct—Columbia and South Carolina was over.

A sketch by J. E. Taylor shows the Thirteenth Iowa Regiment of the Seventeenth Corps raising the Stars and Stripes over the partially completed State House in Columbia. Courtesy of South Caroliniana Library

This Confederate States of America $10 bill, printed at the Confederate Printing Plant at Gervais and Huger streets in Columbia, featured a picture of South Carolina's planned new state capitol. Courtesy of South Caroliniana Library

A sketch by W. Waud of the burning of Columbia on February 17, 1865. The artist is looking down Main Street toward the new State Capitol building. The tall tower on the right was the clock tower of City Hall which extended over the walkway. Courtesy of South Caroliniana Library.

THE WAR COMES HOME

The following nineteen photographs by Brady R. Wearn were taken immediately after Columbia burned on February 17, 1865. The collection, owned by South Caroliniana Library, is printed here for the first time in its entirety. Courtesy of South Caroliniana Library

Looking south down Main Street to the new State Capitol, still under construction.

Looking north up the ravaged Main Street from the Capitol grounds.

The bridge over the Congaree River was burned by Columbians in an attempt to keep General Sherman's troops from reaching the city.

Offices of the South Carolina Railroad were later rebuilt on the same site.

Ebenezer Lutheran Church.

The Presbyterian Church lecture room.

The freight depot of the South Carolina Railroad.

The Evans and Cogswell Printing Plant at Gervais and Huger streets. It was rebuilt and became the State Dispensary.

Catholic Convent at Blanding and Main streets.

The State Armory on Arsenal Hill.

Christ Episcopal Church at Blanding and Marion streets.

Hunt's Hotel.

Ruins of the Clarkson House, home of former Gov. James H. Hammond.

The city jail on Washington Street and the back of the Carolina National Bank.

The corner of Main and Laurel streets.

Dr. Gibbes's home at Sumter and Hampton streets.

Washington Street Methodist Church.

The first block of Main Street facing the Capitol.

Homeless blacks sought places to live among the burned-out ruins of Columbia. A sketch by Theodore R. Davis, courtesy of South Caroliniana Library

The stately columns were all that remained of Gen. Wade Hampton's home on the eastern edge of the city. A new house was built behind the columns, still standing today. Courtesy of South Caroliniana Library

An artist's drawing shows a rebuilt Columbia as seen from Arsenal Hill. The Federal Building is to the left and the new State House, still without a dome, is on the right. Courtesy of South Caroliniana Library

An early photograph of "Tommy" Woodrow Wilson and his family when they lived in Columbia. Courtesy of Historic Columbia Foundation

Rutledge College is the oldest building at the University of South Carolina. This photograph, taken around 1873, is from a glass plate in the USC Archives. Courtesy of the University of South Carolina

Columbia quickly rebuilt after it was devastated in 1865. By the mid-1870s, a number of businesses were operating on Richardson Street, now Main Street. Edwin J. Scott and Bankers was one of the first to reopen. Courtesy of Security Federal Savings and Loan Association

Black coeds studying to be teachers posed outside the Reconstruction University or Normal School started by the University of South Carolina. The school offered a two-year program. Courtesy of McKissick Museum, University of South Carolina

McKenzie's Confectionary, which first opened on Richardson Street before the Civil War, was rebuilt after the burning of Columbia and operated in the city until about 1888. This photograph was taken in the mid-1870s. Courtesy of Security Federal Savings and Loan Association

An artist's sketch of a Reconstruction legislative session. Courtesy of Historic Columbia Foundation

Canvassers gathered outside Carolina Hall, awaiting reports of the vote count being conducted inside. The 1876 election was hotly contested and would mean the end of Reconstruction. Sketch by Harry Ogden, courtesy of South Caroliniana Library

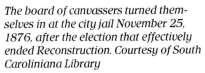

The board of canvassers turned themselves in at the city jail November 25, 1876, after the election that effectively ended Reconstruction. Courtesy of South Caroliniana Library

Wade Hampton III was inaugurated in front of Carolina Hall on December 14, 1876. His election as the state's first Democratic governor since the Civil War signaled the end of Reconstruction. Courtesy of Historic Columbia Foundation

Main St.

"While many new people have come from other States, Columbia is essentially a South Carolina city. Native Columbians are comparatively few but all of the forty-four counties have Columbia colonies. From nearby towns of Winnsboro and Camden, in Fairfield and Kershaw counties, dozens of young men have come to Columbia to enter business life. There is an influential element of Charlestonians here. Columbia is the 'melting pot' of South Carolina, as the United States is of the world, and it is perhaps not risking too much to say that every village of half a thousand people in the State has sent a man or woman, a family or families, to be a part of this capital city and share in its new prosperity."

William Watts Ball
"Columbia of Today" (1913)

THREE
THE FIRST
NEW SOUTH
1877-1920

When the antebellum elite regained control of South Carolina in 1877, they proceeded to manage the state's affairs much as they had prior to 1860—but with one significant difference: Wade Hampton had gained the governorship by appealing to black voters, and he deliberately chose a moderate course in racial matters. His actions at the state level were mirrored by those of his fellow Columbians during the next few years. This conciliatory attitude toward the ex-slaves was motivated by a mixture of honest affection and fear that any repressive acts would resurrect Congressional Reconstruction. Blacks continued to vote and to hold office, but gradually the political gains they had made during Reconstruction were whittled away.

One of Hampton's first acts as governor was to order the closing of his beloved alma mater, the University of South Carolina. In the eyes of most Carolinians, the university, the pride of the state, had been sullied by the Radical Republican regime. The temporary closing of the school seemed to be the only answer. When the college reopened in 1880, it was called the South Carolina College of Agriculture and Mechanic Arts. The legislature provided almost no money for its operation, forcing the administration to depend upon moneys coming from the Morrill Land Grant College Act.

At the Sumter Street entrance to the campus today is a historic marker stating that the university is a "faithful index to the ambitions and fortunes of the state." The phrase just as easily could have said "Columbia" instead of "the state."

During the 1880s, the capital city was described as a "poverty-stricken town of ten thousand." There were no sidewalks or paved streets. When it rained, the roadways became quagmires. When it was dry, the air was filled with dust and grit. Cows freely wandered around town after dark. The southeastern quadrant of the city beyond Green and Pickens streets was still covered with cornfields.

There was a certain amount of defeatism in the air. Could it be that Columbia might be jinxed—that it might never be anything more than a state capital? Scores of young men left town to seek opportunity elsewhere. One Columbian wrote a relative describing the marriage of friends: "It was a pretty wedding but their prospects are very dark." However,

A view of Main Street facing north from the Capitol steps in the 1890s. Courtesy of Security Federal Savings and Loan Association

there were some Columbians who did not yield to their pessimism; they worked hard to make the city more than just a place for entertaining legislators.

During the decade of the 1880s, the city's business community began to stir. The Bell System, in 1880, installed a telephone exchange for sixty-two subscribers. In 1881, the Carolina National Bank was reorganized and placed on a more solid footing. This bank later made possible the completion of the new Columbia Canal and the building of the city's textile mills. The first streetcars, drawn by horses, appeared in 1882.

Improving education was the goal of a number of individuals, but it was not a concern shared by a majority of the voting population. In 1881 and 1882, the citizenry voted down the idea of public schools because taxes would increase. Finally, in 1883, Col. F. W. McMaster and a group of like-minded Columbians convinced taxpayers that the city needed a public school system. A grant from the Peabody Board, a northern philanthropy, helped provide initial funding and the old Columbia Male and Female academies were incorporated into the new school district. Howard School, the city's only black school, had opened in 1867. It would be forty-nine years before the city built another black school. The district's first annual report (1883) noted that there were nine hundred pupils and nineteen teachers in the "Columbia graded schools."

A normal school—as teacher's colleges were called—was an integral part of the legislation creating the Columbia School District. In 1886, Winthrop Training School opened on the grounds of the Columbia Theological Seminary. Later, Ben Tillman and state politics caused it to be moved to Rock Hill.

Another institution of higher education came to town in 1881. Bishop W. F. Dickerson of the African Methodist Episcopal Church was instrumental in having Payne Institute moved from Cokesbury to Columbia. He insisted that the school be renamed Allen University. When some of his associates suggested that the new name might be too pretentious, he said, "Let the school catch up with the name." And it did—over the next seventy-five years, Allen produced the majority of Columbia's black professionals.

Columbia continued to grow following the opening of Allen. The General Assembly voted to renew construction on the unfinished State House, and seven fertilizer plants opened. Between 1884 and 1891, the basic structure of the State House, without porticoes, was completed, and in 1889, the Columbia Phosphate Company was organized to exploit the phosphate deposits found in the lower part of the state. Six other plants soon followed, including two operated by major national companies, Swift and Armor.

The New South fever that gripped certain segments of the community—"Old Columbia will look up yet"—was tempered by a growing nostalgia for the Old South, for the world that had existed before the war and for the Lost Cause of the Confederacy. In 1879, the Confederate Monument on the State House grounds had been dedicated with "the grandest military show" that the city had ever seen.

Socially, the Old South had been revived during the Reconstruction with the formation of the South Carolina Club in 1870. This state-wide organization had its annual ball in Columbia in November. In establishing the club, the old antebellum elite created a social occasion that replaced the annual Commencement Ball at Carolina. After Hampton's victory, the club moved its annual fete from a local meeting hall to the State House.

The membership of the South Carolina Club was state-wide. As the state capital, Columbia shared a number of its organizations with out-of-towners. During the 1880s, however, three strictly local groups came into existence. The Columbia Club (now defunct) came into being in 1884 as "a meeting place for gentlemen." Five years later, a group of women founded The Assembly, at whose annual December ball young ladies made their debuts to Columbia society. In 1891, the Columbia Cotillion Club, a men's organization, was formed to host four dances a year.

It was ironic that the city's elite had closed ranks in the years just preceding the election of "Pitchfork" Ben Tillman of Edgefield County—a man who opposed the very things that they represented. Not only did he overturn the Hampton-led political order, he proceeded to establish a new, negative tone in the state. During his governorship, the "farmer's friend" refused to let the South Carolina Club holds its ball in the State House—but, that would prove to be the least of the things that he did to punish the establishment.

Tillman's 1890 gubernatorial campaign was part of the so-called "Populist Revolt" that had galvanized farmers throughout the country to political action. Falling commodity prices had pushed many to the brink of ruin. The price of South Carolina's cash crop, cotton, had plummeted. In 1869, cotton brought twenty-eight cents a pound. Over the next two decades, increased production only resulted in declining prices. In 1894, cotton brought only about five cents a pound. On the best land in the state, it cost the most efficient farmers six to eight cents a pound to produce. Compounding the problem were the "charges" that farmers had to pay on loans. In some parts of the state the interest ran from 40 percent to 80 percent per annum.

Tillman and his followers had blamed the farmers' plight on those in power. In a vicious campaign, the man from Edgefield triumphed at the polls, but in the process he alienated Columbia and its leadership who remained loyal to Wade Hampton.

One of the most significant results of the 1890 campaign was the decision to establish a newspaper opposing the Tillmanites. In February 1891, the first issue of *The State* appeared. For the next quarter century, it fought Tillman and

The Hill House on Laurel Street Hill was built by Gov. John Taylor in 1793. The house burned 100 years later. This photograph was taken in the early 1880s. Courtesy of South Caroliniana Library

The Columbia veterinary infirmary in the 1880s with Dr. W. Niles. Courtesy of South Caroliniana Library

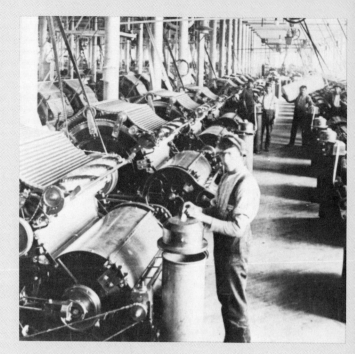

Young children worked in the carding room at the Great Olympia Cotton Mills in the 1890s. Courtesy of South Caroliniana Library

The Governor's Mansion in the early 1890s with Gov. John Gary Evans standing in the left doorway. Courtesy of South Caroliniana Library

his followers at every turn and proved on numerous occasions that the pen was indeed mightier than the sword. The Gonzales brothers took the lead in this enterprise and one of them, N. G., was later murdered by Tillman's nephew—who was lieutenant governor at the time—in the shadow of the State House.

The Tillman years gave *The State* a great deal to write about and Columbians a great deal to talk about. One of the new governor's campaign pledges had been to close down "the seedbed of the aristocracy," the name he gave to the University. Upon his election, he set about creating a new agricultural school in the piedmont "away from the corrupt influences of Columbia." The university's enrollment dwindled, and, had Tillman not had some second thoughts, the school might have closed altogether.

While the dismantling of the university was one of the priorities of Tillman's first administration, the creation of the Dispensary—a state liquor monopoly—was one of the principal acts of his second term. The act creating the Dispensary limited the sale of liquor to state-operated stores. No longer would it be legal to sell whiskey and spirits in taverns, hotels, or drug stores.

The law, needless to say, was not popular in many parts of the state. In Charleston and Columbia, it was flouted openly. A furious governor was determined that the law would be obeyed. His determination and the overzealous conduct of some of his special agents in Darlington resulted in the death of several innocent citizens. A riot ensued in which the agents were hounded into the Pee Dee Swamps.

Governor Tillman, sensing that there was an insurrection brewing, called up the Columbia militia to subdue the rioters. Three companies were called up; none responded. The Richland Volunteers refused to assemble. The Columbia Zouaves threw down their arms. The Governor's Guards wavered until Ellison Capers, former Confederate general and Episcopal Bishop of South Carolina, said if he were an officer in the Guards he would resign rather than respond to the governor's order. The Guards refused the governor's call. *The State* and the local citizenry whole-heartedly applauded the militia's action.

In March and April 1884, Columbia was as tense as it had been in the months between the November 1876 election and the April 1877 withdrawal of federal troops. After the Charleston militia units also refused to heed the governor's call, he turned to his "wool hat boys" from the red hills. When the first of these units reached Columbia, they were met by an angry mob and forced to take refuge behind the walls of the state penitentiary.

Eventually, the governor had his way and order was restored, but he wanted one last word with his "band box soldiers." He summoned the Governor's Guards to the Governor's Mansion for a special reproof and lectured them in rude, earthy terms on their lack of courage and manliness.

He then offered places in the militia to any who would serve him when called upon. Instead of finding the repentance he expected, the astonished governor stood speechless as the guards, to a man, threw down their weapons and left him standing alone on the mansion's steps.

Ben Tillman was in the Governor's Mansion, but Columbians ignored him when they could. In 1891, the city celebrated its centennial on the anniversary of the first meeting of a full session of the General Assembly. There was a two-day holiday, and all businesses closed. Main Street was decorated with arches representing the different counties. And Columbia's own Wade Hampton delivered the principal address.

There was reason for the city to celebrate. It was beginning to break out of the mold of "just being a capital city." The fertilizer factories built in the late 1880s and the opening of the textile mills in the early 1890s seemed to herald an era of industrialization. Henry Grady's "New South" had come to Columbia.

The mills were welcome additions to the city's economy. Built on the outskirts of town, they attracted nearly eight thousand whites from the hardscrabble farms of the piedmont to the banks of the Congaree. The mills were welcome, but the workers lived outside the city limits. With the exception of a settlement house operated by Trinity Episcopal Church, folks who lived in the city mostly ignored those who lived and worked in the mill villages.

The development of the mills—thanks to northern financing—helped give Columbia a prosperous air at the turn of the century. Along Main Street, new shops and stores bustled with local and out-of-town customers. The city had become a major shopping center for people from all over the state. It was easy to get to Columbia by railroad.

Nine rail lines linked the capital with the outside world. The last to enter the city was the Seaboard Airline Railroad. Part of the price that the city paid to attract the line was to sell Sidney Park between Assembly Street and the river. The city used the money to help finance a new city hall, and the railroad turned the park into a rail yard. Tracks entered and crossed the city at various points—a legacy with which Columbians of the 1980s still have to cope—but after 1902 there was one central passenger entry.

For a number of years, the idea of a Union Station had been around, but in January 1902 it became a reality. All across the country cities lavished great sums on monumental structures so that arriving visitors would be impressed. Union Station, looking very much like a French chateau, certainly made for a grand portal to the city.

One new Columbian noticed something else when he arrived at Union Station: segregated waiting rooms. Until Tillman and his followers had seized control of the state, there had been no legal segregation in Columbia or South Carolina. Through the 1895 Constitution and a variety of Jim Crow laws, the Tillmanites created the basis for a segregated society that would last into the 1960s.

Because of segregation, Dr. Mathilda Evans established the Taylor Lane Hospital for blacks. She also operated a free clinic for poor black children. This intrepid woman was a real success story in an age that gloried in them. Not only was she a woman engaged in what was predominantly a male profession, but she was also black. Despite Dr. Evans's uniqueness, very few Columbia whites knew about her or her work. The patterns of a segregated society saw to that—although the famous "Belt Line" trolley ran through Waverly where Dr. Evans was a familiar figure.

The "Belt Line" started on Main Street, ran east on Gervais to Harden and then south on Harden to the Shandon Pavillion near present-day Valley Park. During the summer, there was always a dance band in the wooden Shandon Pavillion on Friday evenings. The trolley ride cost a nickel, and the dances were free. If permitted, young couples might stop off at a Main Street drugstore for a soda on the way home.

Warm summer evenings lent themselves to sitting on the front porches and visiting neighbors. At the turn of the century, Columbians were still talking about the Charleston earthquake of 1886 that had knocked down chimneys in Columbia and scared the daylights out of everyone. The heat of August was contrasted with the "desperate cold" of the winter of 1895 when, for two weeks in February, the mercury did not reach above freezing. The low temperature was four degrees and for the entire period there were nine inches of snow on the ground. Soup kitchens were set up to help the less fortunate, and in Columbia's gardens, roses and sweet olives were killed.

Famous visitors were another favorite topic of conversation. Susan B. Anthony had been warmly received on an 1895 visit as had President Taft in 1909. At a luncheon for Taft in the State House, Columbia's ladies were permitted to sit in the balcony and observe their husbands and fathers eating lunch with the President on the main floor. Booker T. Washington came to town in 1898 and again in 1909. He spoke to black audiences and stayed at the Colonia Hotel, despite Jim Crow laws.

But when Mrs. Stonewall Jackson came to town, the city really rolled out the red carpet. During her 1895 stay, the mayor hosted a gala reception for the widow of one of the Confederacy's greatest heroes.

Summer was also a time for baseball. In 1902, Columbia joined the South Atlantic League. In addition to its professional team, there were dozens of amateur "nines" in all parts of town.

When fall arrived, the weather generally cooled off enough to enjoy indoor entertainment at the theater in the new Columbia City Hall at Main and Gervais streets. Vaudeville was in its heyday, and there were variety shows by the score. On the theater's stage played some of the great names of show business: George M. Cohan, the divine Sarah Bernhardt, all of the Barrymores and Lillian Russell. Victor Herbert's orchestra played in concert and so did John Philip Sousa's band.

Even though the city fathers had built the theater for live performances, a new form of entertainment made its first appearance in 1899. The first movies were shown in Merchants and Manufacturers Hall, and admission was free. By 1910, there were three motion picture theaters: the Grand and Lyric for whites, and the Majestic for blacks.

Segregation had become a way of life in turn-of-the-century Columbia, South Carolina, and much of the rest of the nation. It was one aspect of Columbia's life that progressive citizens did not attempt to alter. Not much else escaped their notice, however. Through a variety of organizations and with the strong support of *The State*, a host of changes occurred.

In 1892, a group of women organized the Columbia Hospital Association. The city gave the association land and this effort became "a community project in the fullest sense." By 1909, all debts had been paid and the ladies relinquished the operation of the hospital to the Columbia Medical Society. In 1914, the South Carolina State Baptist Convention purchased Dr. Augustus B. Knowlton's Infirmary and over the years created a major medical center.

Also in 1914, Ridgewood Camp for the treatment of tuberculosis victims began operation. This worthy cause started as a mission of the Daughters of the Holy Cross of Trinity Episcopal Church, but their efforts soon were matched by other women's church groups. These women were pioneers in working for the treatment of this much feared disease. Before Ridgewood Camp, there was no place in South Carolina that a tuberculosis patient could be treated.

Columbia women also were behind the founding in 1896 of "A Union for Practical Purposes," which later became the Columbia Library Association. This group raised the funds to open the Timrod Library on the second floor of the Loan and Exchange Bank, the city's and the state's first skyscraper, today called the Barringer Building.

Woman suffrage was an important issue of the day in many parts of the country, but it wasn't well-received in South Carolina. In 1919, the General Assembly refused to ratify the nineteenth amendment giving women the right to vote, but it became law anyway.

Columbia's men didn't leave civic improvements entirely to their mothers, sisters, and wives. The Civic Improvement League hired a New Yorker, who in 1905 published a report of "The Value of Beauty to a City." In it, he detailed plans that called for the purchase of fountains and statuary, and the planting of trees and flowers. References were made to the beauty of Rome and Paris—and of Columbia's comparable potential.

The city fathers ignored the plan's recommendation that the streets remain unpaved. In 1907, paving began on the

sixteen blocks of Main Street from Union Station to Elmwood. The material used was not very satisfactory, and in warm weather horses, wheels, and shoes left their imprints. Wooden blocks were tried on Washington and Hampton streets, but they were replaced after a few years of buckling, swelling, and floating away during thunderstorms.

The decision to install the wooden streets had been one of the first ones made by a new city government. Progressives across the country wanted to take "bossism" out of local politics. There wasn't a machine in Columbia, but a form of government that included ward representation was considered to be too easy to corrupt. In 1910, by a vote of 1,310 to 68, Columbians adopted a new government with a mayor and city commissioner. Wade Hampton Gibbes was the first mayor elected under the new system.

Voters also approved the 1913 annexation of Shandon, Waverly, South Waverly, and a portion of Eau Claire; and a 1915 school bond issue. The bond issue paid for the new Columbia High, Logan, and Booker T. Washington schools.

One of the city's best known assets didn't cost the taxpayers a dime. Despite President Woodrow Wilson's public assurances of neutrality during the early years of World War I, a group of Columbians purchased twelve hundred acres northeast of town which they turned over to the federal government to be used as an army training facility. When war came in 1917, Camp Jackson was established and within a year

some seventy thousand young men were in training there.

Columbians had a very special feeling about President Woodrow Wilson. They considered him to be one of their own who had gone from the house on the corner of Hampton and Henderson streets to the White House. Wilson's father had been a faculty member of the Columbia Theological Seminary. Young Tommy, as he was known, spent his formative teenage years in Reconstruction Columbia before going off to Davidson College in North Carolina. Wilson never forgot his Columbia connections and visited the town on several occasions.

When he led the nation into war "to make the world safe for democracy," hundreds of young Columbians responded to their country's call. Churches operated recreation centers, and the Community Club fed thousands of soldiers. The city's women had the primary responsibility for staffing these outreach facilities, yet many still found the time to roll bandages for the Red Cross.

The "war to end all wars" was over in November 1918, and most of Columbia's boys came home. Wilson was still President, but there wasn't much local interest in his League of Nations or the Treaty of Versailles. They were part of one crusade too many. The war seemed to have taken the steam out of the progressive impulse that had gripped the city (and the nation) for nearly two decades.

A horse-drawn streetcar in the early 1890s. By 1900, all the streetcars were powered by electricity. Courtesy of South Carolina Electric & Gas Co.

The Hotel Congaree, billed as "head-quarters for the traveling man," cost one dollar a day in the 1890s. The hotel, which ceased to operate between 1915 and 1920, was located on Gervais and Assembly streets. Courtesy of Security Federal Savings and Loan Association

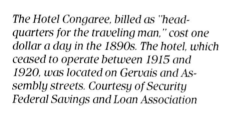

Supreme Court Justice Henry McIver, Chief Justice W. D. Simpson and Justice Samuel McGowan posed in 1887 in the South Carolina Supreme Court chambers. The photograph was taken by Columbian Dr. John M. McBryde. Courtesy of South Caroliniana Library

An exterior view of the Columbia Coca-Cola Bottling Company's plant around the turn of the century. Courtesy of South Caroliniana Library

The C. H. Baldwin fine groceries store operated on Main Street in the late 1880s. Courtesy of South Caroliniana Library

Students posing outside the original Columbia High School at Washington and Marion streets in the late 1800s. Courtesy of South Caroliniana Library

An interior view of the Capitol City Cafe around the turn of the century. Courtesy of South Caroliniana Library

The Columbia College building that burned in 1964 is seen in this 1910 photograph. The trolley car ran to the college's front door. Courtesy of Security Federal Savings and Loan Association

Sixth graders at Washington Street Graded School pose for a class picture in 1893. Courtesy of South Caroliniana Library

A photograph of the State Capitol building under construction in 1885. The building was started in 1855, and thirty years later it still had a temporary roof. Courtesy of Security Federal Savings and Loan Association

The staff of The Columbia Register, which published from 1875 to 1898, outside the Main Street office. Courtesy of Security Federal Savings and Loan Association

Mme Sosnowski and "her girls" at the South Carolina Collegiate Institute in May 1888. Courtesy of South Caroliniana Library

The Columbia Market, along Assembly Street, was built after the Civil War and razed in 1913. Courtesy of Security Federal Savings and Loan Association

A vaudeville troupe drives up an unpaved Main Street in the 1890s. The municipal opera house is on the second and third floors of the twin-towered City Hall at Washington and Main streets. Courtesy of Security Federal Savings and Loan Association

M. H. Berry, a Main Street store selling everything from baby buggies and furniture to shoes, celebrated forty-eight years of business in 1891. The store has no known connection to the current Berry's stores in Columbia. Courtesy of Security Federal Savings and Loan Association

American soldiers marching down Main Street shortly after the Spanish-American War. Courtesy of Security Federal Savings and Loan Association

The Allen University Class of 1892. Courtesy of Columbia Newspapers Inc.

The 1600 and 1700 blocks of Main Street between 1893 and 1907. C. H. Baldwin grocery story and Globe Dry Goods are in the right foreground. Courtesy of Security Federal Savings and Loan Association

Nurses at the State Insane Asylum with one of the doctors in 1895. Courtesy of South Caroliniana Library

Two coeds relax on the lawn of the University of South Carolina Horseshoe in 1899. Women were first admitted to the school in 1894. Courtesy of the University of South Carolina

A wood-burning train pulling up at the Columbia train station. Apparently a special train for a special occasion, the second car is draped with banners and marked "Governor's Guards," a Columbia militia unit. Courtesy of Security Federal Savings and Loan Association

Workers at the South Carolina Penitentiary Boot and Shoe Factory stand outside the store around the 1900s. Courtesy of Security Federal Savings and Loan Association

The South Carolina Presbyterian Institute for young ladies, founded in 1886, was photographed in 1890. It was bought by a self-perpetuating board in 1910 and the name was changed to The South Carolina College for Women. After attempts to merge with the University of South Carolina failed, the college merged with Chicora College of Greenville, but continued to operate in Columbia. In 1930, the college merged with Queens College in Charlotte, North Carolina, and moved to that city. Courtesy of South Caroliniana Library

North Main Street, at the turn of the century, featured wooden storage buildings and blacksmith shops. Courtesy of Security Federal Savings and Loan Association

The State newspaper, founded in 1891, occupied this building on Main Street in 1897. By 1905, the building had tripled in size. Courtesy of Security Federal Savings and Loan Association

Columbia's second City Hall, at Main and Washington streets, was built in 1874 and burned in 1899. Courtesy of South Caroliniana Library

Workers at the South Carolina Dispensary in the 1890s. Courtesy of South Caroliniana Library

Children working in the spinning room at the Olympia Cotton Mills in 1903. Courtesy of South Caroliniana Library

Students of Allen Graded School at the turn of the century. From the Biggs family album, courtesy of South Caroliniana Library

The intersection of Main and Hampton
streets between 1905 and 1910. Sylvan
Brothers jewelry store, right, has been at
the location since 1900. Courtesy of
Security Federal Savings and Loan
Association

The Great Flood of 1908 left the Power House on the Columbia Canal partially submerged. Courtesy of South Caroliniana Library

The interior of Leevy's Department Store around 1910. Courtesy of South Caroliniana Library

Trinity Episcopal Church choir, Easter Day, 1906. Courtesy of South Caroliniana Library

The Wade Hampton Gibbes house, a typical Columbia cottage, is shown before it was moved to make way for a new street in 1904. The house, built in 1867, would have been demolished, as it was located in the middle of what became College Street. Courtesy of South Caroliniana Library

Employees at work in the Southern Railway Freight Office, July 6, 1908. Courtesy of South Caroliniana Library

The Gervais Street bridge across the
Congaree River at the high water mark of
thirty-six feet, August 1908. The bridge
was a toll bridge until 1912. Courtesy of
South Caroliniana Library

The Palmetto Building, across Washington
Street from the Barringer building, was
under construction in 1912 and 1913. The
roof of the former Richland County Courthouse is in the foreground. Courtesy of
Security Federal Savings and Loan
Association

Motormen and conductors of the street railway system standing at the transfer station at Main and Gervais streets in 1914. Courtesy of Security Federal Savings and Loan Association

The steeple of the First Presbyterian Church was photographed on fire, 3:30 A.M., February 22, 1910. Courtesy of Security Federal Savings and Loan Association

A lightning storm over downtown Columbia, August 19, 1912. Courtesy of Security Federal Savings and Loan Association

A painting shows the University of South Carolina campus around 1910. Longstreet Theater, right, was built in 1855. Courtesy of South Caroliniana Library

The 1800 block of Main Street around 1910. The steeple of the Main Street United Methodist Church can be seen in the background. Courtesy of Security Federal Savings and Loan Association

The Columbia Canal, during the flood of 1910, overflowed its banks. The State Penitentiary can be seen on the left, and the pumphouse is on the site of the Riverfront Park. Courtesy of South Caroliniana Library

Mimnaugh's department store, at Main and Hampton streets, was on the present-day site of Belk's department store. Courtesy of Security Federal Savings and Loan Association

J. D. Perry Fresh Meats operated at the 1900 block of Main Street around 1910. The side of the store served as a billboard for advertisements. Courtesy of Security Federal Savings and Loan Association

A photograph taken between 1909 and 1917 shows Roddey Automobile Company and its inventory of cars for sale. Courtesy of Security Federal Savings and Loan Association

W. H. Donly Fancy Groceries at Elmwood Avenue and Main Street had advertisements on the side wall for products such as Merita bread, Rose's "Purity" Whiskey and White Rose tea. Courtesy of Security Federal Savings and Loan Association

Columbia's Police and Fire departments—and all their equipment—lined up in front of the State House steps for a photograph in the fall of 1910. The banner across Main Street promotes Flying Machines at the State Fair Grounds. Courtesy of Security Federal Savings and Loan Association

Another view of Columbia, taken about
1912, from the top of the water tower on
Arsenal Hill, shows downtown Columbia.
Laurel Hill, home of Edwin Wales Robert-
son, is in the foreground and Seaboard
Park, formerly Sidney Park, is on the right.
Courtesy of Security Federal Savings and
Loan Association

A photograph taken about 1912 from the
top of the water tank on Arsenal Hill looks
northeast across Elmwood Avenue. The
row of houses in the foreground were at
Assembly and Richland streets, and the
land across Elmwood Avenue was all farm-
land. Courtesy of Security Federal Savings
and Loan Association

An electric streetcar traveling through the Eau Claire section of Columbia in the early 1900s. Courtesy of Security Federal Savings and Loan Association

The entire Sheriff's Department astride their horses on the 1400 block of Sumter Street in 1913. Courtesy of Security Federal Savings and Loan Association

The Confederate Soldiers Home at Bull Street and Confederate Avenue was open until the mid twentieth century. Courtesy of Security Federal Savings and Loan Association

87

Citizens gathered for the dedication of Columbia City Hall and Theater at Main and Gervais streets in the early 1900s. Courtesy of South Caroliniana Library

M. Ehrlich & Sons shoe store did business in Columbia in the early 1900s. A variety of shoe stores, all including the Ehrlich name, had operated in the city since before the Civil War. Courtesy of Security Federal Savings and Loan Association

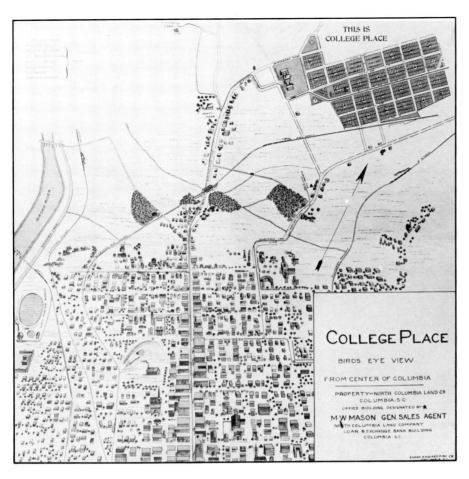

A 1910 map shows College Place, which developed around Columbia College, as seen from the center of downtown. The map was prepared for the North Columbia Land Company. Courtesy of South Caroliniana Library

Soldiers lined up for inspection at Camp Jackson during World War I. Courtesy of South Caroliniana Library

A snowstorm in 1910 blanketed downtown Columbia. The National Loan and Exchange Building, the state's first skyscraper, left, is at Main and Washington streets. Courtesy of Security Federal Savings and Loan Association

Horse-drawn wagons bringing cotton to the cotton market on Gervais Street in early 1900s. In the background, a train can be seen blocking traffic. Courtesy of Security Federal Savings and Loan Association

The new steel building, at the entrance to the South Carolina State Fair Grounds, was built about 1912. Rosewood Drive, seen in the foreground, still had not been paved. Courtesy of Security Federal Savings and Loan Association

Miss Mamie Boozer, right, with her students outside Olympia School in 1903. Streetcar tracks ran in front of the school. Courtesy of Columbia Newspapers Inc.

Columbia children riding in a goat-drawn cart around 1910. Courtesy of South Caroliniana Library

The Richland County Courthouse, shown about 1900, was at Washington and Sumter streets. Courtesy of Security Federal Savings and Loan Association

Who the people are in this photograph is disputed by historians. Some believe they are soldiers training for the Spanish-American War, while other historians think the picture was taken in the early 1900s and shows participants in a rifle contest. The men were standing in front of the auditorium of Hyatt Park at North Main Street and Monticello Road. Courtesy of Security Federal Savings and Loan Association

Workers at the Columbia streetcar repair shop on the 300 block of Main Street are shown around 1900. Courtesy of South Carolina Electric & Gas Co.

Utility company employees at work in the drafting room at Main and Tobacco (Catawba) streets. Courtesy of South Carolina Electric & Gas Co.

South Carolina Governor Richard I. Manning, who served from 1915 to 1919, sits on a horse outside the Governor's Mansion. The flag with its five stars represents his five sons fighting in World War I. A sixth son later joined the service, and one of his sons was killed. Courtesy of Security Federal Savings and Loan Association

Soldiers lining up to wash their mess kits after a meal at Camp Jackson during World War I. Courtesy of the U.S. Army

University of South Carolina students surveyed the Gibbes Green area of campus in 1915. The area is behind the present-day McKissick Museum. Courtesy of the University of South Carolina

The original Maxcy Gregg House, a classic Columbia cottage, was photographed in 1906, shortly before the porch was expanded and dormer windows were added to the second floor. The house, a Greek Revival design, was built in 1841 and is in the 1500 block of Richland Street. Courtesy of Columbia Newspapers Inc.

Columbia artist Blondell Malone (1879-
1951) outside her house at 1517 Gervais
Street. Courtesy of South Caroliniana
Library

Miss Malone posing in her graciously
appointed home in 1909. Courtesy of
South Caroliniana Library

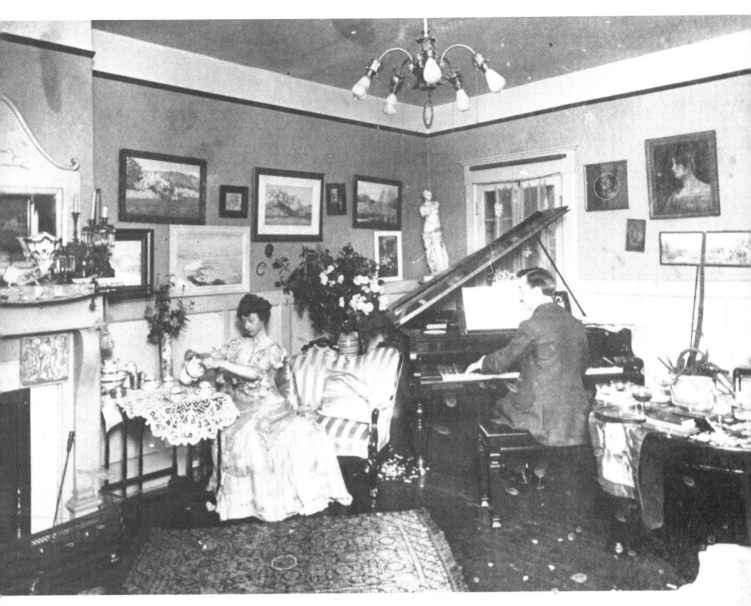

Blondell Malone entertaining a visitor in her parlor in 1909. Courtesy of South Caroliniana Library

Students at the College for Women in 1914, in their tennis garb, ready to play. Courtesy of South Caroliniana Library

Convicts, in prison stripes, working on the road at Williams and Hampton streets in the 1920s. Courtesy of South Carolina Electric & Gas Co.

Crews laid rails for streetcars at Gervais and Sumter streets in the early 1900s. Courtesy of South Carolina Electric & Gas Co.

Utility company employees set poles for electrical wires at Gervais and Marion streets in 1912. Courtesy of South Carolina Electric & Gas Co.

Repair work was done along Gervais Street in 1912 by crews from the utility company. Courtesy of South Carolina Electric & Gas Co.

A streetcar crosses Rocky Branch to enter the car barn at 328 South Main Street in 1912. Although the car barn is gone today, the building to its left is still standing. Courtesy of South Carolina Electric & Gas Co.

A photograph taken between 1910 and 1920 shows cotton fields in the foreground and Gervais Street and the Mount Vernon Mill in the background. Courtesy of South Carolina Electric & Gas Co.

The University of South Carolina Glee Club in 1905 with their instruments. Courtesy of the University of South Carolina

A streetcar, around 1900 vintage, is shown on a Columbia street. Courtesy of South Carolina Electric & Gas Co.

Morris & Son, a stone crushing plant, operated in Columbia about the turn of the century. Courtesy of the City of Columbia

The Colonia Hotel, about the turn of the century, served twice as the home of Columbia College. Courtesy of South Caroliniana Library

*Columbians posing with an early
Columbia city fire truck. Courtesy of the
City of Columbia*

*Regal Drug Store, offering prescriptions
by pharmacists, operated in Columbia
around the turn of the century. Courtesy of
Columbia Newspapers Inc.*

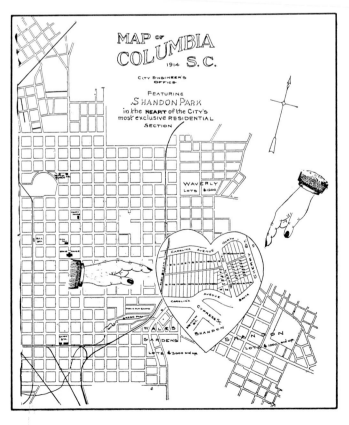

Shandon, in the early 1900s, was farm houses and rolling fields. This photograph was taken looking toward Devine Street from the intersection of Wheat and Holly streets. Courtesy of Historic Columbia Foundation

A 1914 real estate map of Columbia shows Shandon Park, "the heart of the city's most exclusive residential section." Courtesy of South Caroliniana Library

"Columbia's outstanding, incomparable asset is in that
Spirit of Columbia which has entered into the hearts of so
many of the men and women who have come here, to
make a city of homes, where 'good neighbors' live. Not
only have they entered into the life of the city, but they
have contributed tremendous motive power which has
driven through the notable accomplishments. They have
given inspiration to development in the higher spheres
of life."

William Elliott Gonzales
"Foreword" to *Columbia:
Capital City of South Carolina* (1936)

FOUR
ONLY
YESTERDAY
1920-1970

Columbians seemed to have only one thing in mind after the war was over: "a determination to get all the pleasure possible out of life." In this desire to have fun, Columbians were quite in step with folks all over America.

Entertainment took a variety of forms. In 1920, Town Theatre began remodeling an old residence on Sumter Street for its playhouse, and four years later when that proved not to be big enough, a brick theater was built. This little theater, the oldest in the country, thrived despite tremendous competition from movie houses and out-of-town stars such as Will Rogers. The Oklahoma cowboy twice visited the city during the 1920s and wowed his standing-room-only audiences with his homespun humor. In 1929, radio station WBRW began weekly broadcasts, and the following year WIS radio went on the air. Columbians were now able to hear in their living rooms what they formerly had to go downtown to see.

And, in the privacy of their homes, many otherwise law-abiding Columbians ignored Prohibition. Some made their own bathtub gin, while others patronized bootleggers who either made their own or sold liquor smuggled in from the Bahamas. Bluff Road became notorious in local lore as the scene of many a high-speed automobile chase between federal agents and local moonshiners.

Cars seemed to be everywhere. As a result, moves were made to pave the city's residential streets as well as those in the commercial district. Despite a concentrated effort, by the 1930s only 41 out of 152 miles of city streets were paved. But never mind, Columbians loved their cars. Instead of hiring a carriage with a driver for dances, they drove themselves. Automobiles wrought considerable change in social customs and traditions, but there were some things that were impervious to change.

The older social organizations continued to hold formal balls and forbid any of the "new" dance steps. The post-college crowd, however, could do the Charleston and the bunny hug at the newly-formed Tarantella Club's three yearly dances. And for younger Columbians, an invitation to the Germans, a popular club at the University, continued to be an attraction.

Black Columbians formed their own social groups. Social segregation mirrored the rigid racial lines that had been established since the turn of the century.

Farmers pulled their trucks up to the curbside to hawk their truckloads of cantaloupes and watermelons at the market on Assembly Street in the 1940s. Courtesy of South Caroliniana Library

There were even two separate state fairs.

Fair Week in October was the biggest single source of entertainment. From all across South Carolina, friends and relatives descended upon the capital city, and for a full week Columbia became one giant party. And, not so coincidentally, a surprising number of organizations managed to stage meetings in town during Fair Week.

Main Street became a midway with side shows and food booths stretching for blocks. The trolley cars ran to the fairgrounds, making it easy for visitors to see the agricultural exhibits and then ride downtown for some fun and entertainment.

The biggest attraction of the week was Big Thursday, the annual football game between the University of South Carolina and Clemson. The first game was held in 1896—with Carolina winning 12-6—but because of violence the series had been banned by the General Assembly in 1902. Reinstituted in 1909, it grew in importance, until by the 1920s, it had become more than merely a gridiron clash between state rivals. The Carolina-Clemson Game was a major social and political event.

The good times were supported by a prosperity that seemed as though it would last forever. The war provided a big temporary boost to Columbia's economy, but the growth continued even after Camp Jackson was closed. Between 1910 and 1920 the city's population had increased 42 percent, from 26,300 to 37,600. It would grow by another 37 percent during the decade of the 1920s. Everywhere there was concrete evidence that Columbia was prospering.

Public and private building occurred at a rapid pace. The federal government built a new post office on Gervais Street and the state government built its first office building, the Calhoun Building, behind the Capitol on Senate Street. The city's school district had three separate bond issues approved for new buildings. A new auditorium, The Township, was started in 1929 as was Owens Field, Columbia's first airport.

In the private sector, there were major real estate developments: Forest Hills, Hollywood, and Five Points. Benedict College erected a new science building. New sanctuaries were built by Rose Hill Presbyterian, Shandon Lutheran (now Incarnation), St. Peter's Roman Catholic, College Place Methodist and Bethel African Methodist Episcopal churches. Downtown, Trinity Episcopal, First Presbyterian and Washington Street Methodist churches constructed new church school buildings.

By far the most impressive construction project of the decade was the building of what would later be called the Lake Murray dam. It took three years to complete the dam and power station on the Saluda River above the city. In addition, this $20 million project by the Lexington Power Company created a magnificent recreational lake, the potential of which was not fully realized for years.

The physical growth of the city was matched by the development of private organizations whose sole purposes were civic improvement. Businessmen formed the Columbia Kiwanis and Rotary clubs which served as forums for discussion and information. The city's women formed the Columbia Women's Club and the Junior League to do their part in making Columbia a better place in which to live. In an effort to promote the concept of a beautiful city as well as a fast-growing one, the Columbia Garden Club was formed. The idea was attractive and soon other garden clubs blossomed all over town.

New buildings, a burgeoning population, lots of fun things to do—Columbia seemed to be right in step with the rest of the country during the "Roaring Twenties." What folks didn't talk about much over the new dial telephones—installed in 1922—were the warning signals hidden beneath the prosperity, that all was not well with the state's or the nation's economies.

Falling cotton prices and the destructive boll weevil brought depression to rural South Carolina a decade before the rest of the country. Farm foreclosures were all too common, as were bank failures. During the three-year period from 1922 to 1924, ninety South Carolina banks failed. Among them were four Columbia financial institutions.

The bank failures of the 1920s were but a preview of what was to come. The onset of the Great Depression hit South Carolina hard. Columbia, however, was better insulated than either Charleston or Greenville because it was "essentially a government city."

There might have been some insulation, but thousands living in the capital city struggled to survive. Even the presence of the state government was no great asset. When the state treasury didn't have enough funds to pay its bills, state employees received state-issued scrip instead of real money. Local merchants who accepted scrip promptly discounted it so that state employees in effect took a salary cut. One dinner guest in the home of a distinguished university professor commented on his host's family furniture and antique silver. When dinner came, the main course was Spam—served on a silver waiter—as if it were a standing rib roast!

Life was not as humorous for the carpenter who earned $15.00 a week or the female mill worker who earned $12.50 or the black domestic who earned $3.00. Their weekly wages barely covered the necessities of life—when they could get employment. One unemployed Columbian told of a Christmas during the Depression: "Saturday I took the children uptown to see Santa Claus. That was all we could do, just see. None of them pretty Christmas things showing in the windows was for us."

Local charities simply could not cope with the problems resulting from the collapse of the country's economy. It was not until the election of Franklin D. Roosevelt and the enactment of his New Deal programs that assistance was

Bon Air School, which operated from 1896 to 1931, was a unique private school located near the University of South Carolina campus. This class photo is from the 1920s. Courtesy of Mrs. William N. Geiger

Four winners of the Columbia High School Typing Contest posed with their trophies in 1924. Courtesy of South Caroliniana Library

provided for those in need. Virtually every one of the New Deal's agencies had a state headquarters in Columbia. The city benefited greatly from the presence of these agencies. but in some cases they financed major construction projects.

These construction projects provided the University with new dormitories, the McKissick Library and Carolina Stadium; the state with the Wade Hampton State Office Building; and the city with the Veterans' Hospital and the new Farmers' Market sheds on Assembly Street. These sheds proved to be a real boon to the city's economy.

Columbia was able to reinforce its position as one of the major regional market and shipping points for farm produce. From all over the South, corn, beans, sweet potatoes, watermelons, and other truck crops arrived at the market by truck and mule-drawn wagon. Most of the produce left by refrigerated rail car for the eastern markets. The farmers and shippers who came to the market also helped Columbia's not-so-secret red-light district on Gates (Park) Street flourish.

The Gates Street brothels were below Assembly and therefore out of sight of the local housewives who frequented the market. Although there were corner grocery stores in almost every neighborhood, the Farmers' Market was considered the place to get the freshest vegetables. During the spring and summer months, many a Columbia matron trekked to the market with a wide-brimmed hat on her head and a basket on her arm.

Shopping at the Farmers' Market was strictly a cash-and-carry expedition. No credit was available. For those without any cash, there was federal poor relief or possible employment on a federal project.

Camp Jackson, which was deactivated after World War I and turned over to the South Carolina National Guard as a training facility, provided transient housing for some in the mid-1930s.

The massive infusion of federal aid helped the city and its people weather the depression. Unfortunately, the same could not be said for a number of local institutions.

In addition to the banks and businesses that failed, Columbia lost Chicora College which occupied the old Hampton-Preston Mansion on Blanding Street. For forty years known as the South Carolina Presbyterian Institute for young ladies, later as the College for Women and finally as Chicora College, the school had been an important part of the city's cultural life. Financial instability, caused by the depression, led to Chicora's merger with Queens College in Charlotte.

Despite all of the failures and closings, Columbians decided that they would celebrate the 150th anniversary of their city's founding with a huge birthday party. Under the energetic leadership of state Senator James H. Hammond, the Sesquicentennial Commission sponsored a variety of festivities in 1936. There were pageants, speeches, visiting dignitaries and parades. Richland County began construction of a new courthouse into which a time capsule was inserted that was opened during the city's Bicentennial.

Not all of the Sesquicentennial Celebration was hoopla, however. The Commission appointed a historical committee under the capable leadership of Mrs. Julian Hennig. That group produced *Columbia: Capital City of South Carolina, 1786-1936*, the only real "history" of the city ever done. Although a half-century old, the book is still a sound reference work for those interested in Columbia's past.

The publishing of the history of Columbia was one of two major legacies of the Sesquicentennial. The other was the purchase of land beyond the northeastern edge of town for a public park. Today Sesquicentennial Park is a monument for the foresight of its founders, as it is surrounded by the rapidly developing northeastern section of the city.

While the Sesquicentennial Celebration involved many

A Columbia drugstore in the early 1920s
sported a new dial telephone. Courtesy of
South Caroliniana Library

Columbians, it ignored 38 percent of the city's population. In the midst of the festivities, *The Palmetto Leader*, a black newspaper, published an editorial that noted black contributions to the city. Chief among these was the black labor that had built Columbia. In addition, the editors commented, "No city of the South has a better record for fair and just treatment of the weaker element than Columbia, and as a result the race relation is and always has been of the best." The moderate tone of *The Palmetto Leader* would change in a decade when young black Columbians returned from World War II.

In 1940 the federal government reactivated Camp Jackson as Fort Jackson and soon tens of thousands of young men were training among the pine and scrub oak that covered the reservation's sand hills.

The fort and the war attracted new people and new businesses. Between 1940 and 1950, the city's population jumped 39 percent from 62,300 to 86,900. Many of these new residents first came to town because of Fort Jackson and the Columbia Army Air Base across the river.

The streets of the city were thronged with young men in khaki. There was an acute housing shortage as families came to live near their men at the fort. Prices for everyday items such as pickled sausages rose from two-for-a-nickel to ten cents each—if you could get them. The pace of life picked up, even with the heat.

There was a job to be done. Victory gardens sprouted all over town. The state's First Lady, Mrs. R. M. Jefferies, was photographed in the kitchen of the Governor's Mansion flattening cans for a scrap drive. Other housewives did the same. Columbians were willing and eager to do their part for the war effort.

Little did they or anyone else know how important the city and its two major military installations were to the country and its allies. At the Columbia Army Air Base, Col.

Jimmy Doolittle recruited and trained his crews for the famous Tokyo bombing raid. Thirty-five miles further south in the town of North, pilots and bombardiers learned to use the bombsight that would enable them to drop their bombs on Nazi German targets with pinpoint accuracy. The roar of planes overhead on training flights became an accepted part of Columbia life.

Columbians also became accustomed to the thud of exploding shells and the static of machine-gun fire from the training at Fort Jackson. The fort was one of the army's major infantry training bases. In 1942, the United States War Department brought British Prime Minister Winston Churchill to Fort Jackson to see firsthand the capabilities of America's fighting men.

Because of wartime security, the world did not learn that the Prime Minister had been at the fort until after his safe return to England. During his visit on June 24 he saw for the first time an airborne assault and was much impressed with the men and their training. He also was impressed with the area. It was a hot summer day which he said reminded him of the plains of India.

For five years, men from all over the country traveled to Columbia to train at Fort Jackson. When the war was over, there were indications that the fort would be deactivated once more, but it was needed when the Korean Conflict began in 1950, and has remained in use since. In 1964, a major twenty-year building program began replacing the temporary wooden World War II structures with modern brick and concrete buildings. Four years later, the eighty-two-square-mile military reservation was incorporated into the Columbia city limits.

In 1950, the fort remained and the city's population had grown to 86,900. For the first time in its history, Columbia was the largest city in the state, moving ahead of Charleston

Youths attending daily vacation Bible School at the First Baptist Church in June 1926 gathered on the front steps for a group picture. Courtesy of South Caroliniana Library

which for 180 years had been the largest.

This tremendous growth made it difficult to govern under the old city commission. In September 1949, the city's voters had approved a council-manager form of government. The following June five councilmen (including a mayor) were elected. They, in turn, hired a professional administrator to oversee the day-to-day operations of the city. The National Municipal League named Columbia an "All-American City" in 1951 with the new government being cited as one of the reasons the city had been selected.

There were other kinds of "progress," too, but the kind that most Columbians would just as soon forget. For nearly a decade, they neglected to plan for the future or consider the past. The stately residential neighborhoods east of Sumter Street in the old central city succumbed to urban blight, encroaching commercial districts, or the wrecking ball. Although many of the city's landmarks disappeared after World War II, there were two important ones that did not.

In 1949, the Taylor House on Senate Street became the permanent home of the Columbia Museum of Art. The Columbia Art Association now had a place to display the collections it had assembled over the years. Then, through the efforts of native Columbian David Finlay, Director of the National Gallery of Art, a portion of the Kress Collection of Renaissance art was donated to the new museum.

Another building that would become one of the city's major cultural assets was the Ainsley Hall House on Blanding Street. Designed by Robert Mills, this stately structure had fallen on hard times and was scheduled for demolition. A group of concerned Columbians banded together to save what is today known as the Robert Mills Historic House. In almost a classic example of similar preservation efforts across

the country, Mable Payne, the city's preservation officer, fended off the bulldozers with a shotgun until the officers of the Historic Columbia Foundation arrived with the necessary funds to pay off the wrecking crew and the owners. Over the next few years, the Foundation raised more than $1 million to purchase, restore, and furnish the Mills House.

While the Taylor and Mills houses were becoming important local assets, Columbia lost two very different cultural attractions. The Farmers' Market, with the large crowds it attracted, was considered to be a nuisance by downtown merchants. During the 1950s, it was moved from its historic Assembly Street site to Bluff Road. Thirty years later a group of Columbians, charged with helping the city focus on its cultural heritage, lamented the removal of the market from its original location because it had contributed greatly to the city's identity as a central market town for the entire state.

The other cultural loss occurred when Clemson notified the University and the State Fair that after 1960 it would no longer participate in Big Thursday. Since its renewal in 1909, the game had become more important than "who was to be governor, or the establishment of a $1 million enterprise." Instead it became simply a home-and-home football series, and the South, the state, and Columbia had lost a part of their heritage.

The changes and developments of the post-war years were beginning to concern many residents. In the late 1950s, the Chamber of Commerce decided to ask Columbians to suggest ways to improve their city. Questionnaires were distributed in grocery stores. From the responses it received, the chamber developed a series of priorities. So did Lester Bates, an insurance man turned politician. Bates ran for

mayor on a "Ten Point Program for Progress." His program was remarkably similar to the priorities that had emerged from the answers to the chamber's questionnaire.

Citizen committees, comprised mainly of newcomers to the city, were formed. Between 1960 and 1965, some twenty-two new plants employing five thousand people were built. A new $7.5 million jetport was opened in Lexington County. These new businesses and improvements were attracted to Columbia because of its central location, inexpensive utilities, and favorable labor climate. Although a lot of other southern towns could offer the same attributes, Columbia could offer something extra—political and social stability.

The Civil Rights Movement was gathering all over the South. In 1961, there was a street demonstration in Columbia involving about two hundred students. All along Main Street, there were stores with segregated restrooms, dressing rooms, water fountains, and lunch counters. Some restaurants and theaters did not admit blacks at all.

If the Capital City were going to avoid the violence and racial strife afflicting other southern cities, then something had to be done. In 1963, Mayor Bates called together about sixty leading businessmen to discuss the problem. This group, in turn, selected eighteen of their number to be a "secret committee" to work toward the desegregation of the city.

At first, the changes were slow, but they were unmistakable. The "white only" and "colored only" signs disappeared from businesses as theater, hotel, and restaurant owners quietly dropped their segregationist policies. The University of South Carolina desegregated peacefully in 1963—a marked contrast to the confrontations at the University of Alabama and the University of Mississippi. In the fall of 1964, formerly all-white public schools admitted

two dozen black students. Throughout the transition from a segregated to a desegregated city, the Mayor worked closely with black and white leaders to achieve his goal of a peaceful solution.

In 1965 Columbia was once again chosen as an "All-American City." The improvement in race relations, the development of the Columbia Museum of Art, the passage of a new zoning ordinance, and the recognition of the importance of historic preservation were among the reasons listed for the city's being selected. In national magazines—*Look, Coronet* and *Newsweek*—Columbia was hailed as a city of the New South. The changes wrought in the city had been the result of careful planning.

After almost a decade of relatively unplanned growth in the 1950s, Columbians had gone on a planning binge during the 1960s. In 1961, the Columbia City Planning Commission issued a report entitled "In Step with Tomorrow." Four years later appeared "Citizens' Design for Progress," a study drawn up by a blue-ribbon panel of business, government, and civic leaders. One of their concerns was increasing traffic congestion, and this problem was addressed in the 1966 Columbia Area Transportation Study (popularly called the COATS plan).

The most elaborate plan of the decade resulted from a study of the viability of the downtown area by Constantinos Doxiadis in cooperation with local architects, planners, and engineers. This study, called the Doxiadis Plan, was presented to the city by the Chamber of Commerce in December 1969 as a planning blueprint for Columbia for the remainder of the twentieth century.

Two ladies pushing babies in prams through a typical downtown residential neighborhood in the 1920s. Courtesy of Security Federal Savings and Loan Association

Columbians gathered en masse on October 9, 1929, to see the city's first showing of an electric Kelvinator refrigerator. Courtesy of South Carolina Electric & Gas Co.

The first University of South Carolina Uniformed Band, organized in 1923-24 and directed by Professor G. E. Olson, had twenty members. Courtesy of the University of South Carolina

A one-room schoolhouse for blacks was photographed April 28, 1930. Courtesy of South Carolina Electric & Gas Co.

Town Theatre, the longest continually running community theater in the United States, was housed in temporary quarters from 1921-23. Courtesy of South Caroliniana Library

The First Baptist Church, one of Columbia's few downtown buildings not destroyed when the city burned, is shown in the 1930s. Courtesy of South Caroliniana Library

The interior of the First Presbyterian Church before the old pews were replaced. Courtesy of South Caroliniana Library

Edgar Wallace Biggs and some friends posed after a rabbit hunt. From the Biggs family album, courtesy of South Caroliniana Library

Confederate Memorial Day, in the late 1920s, meant decorations at the foot of the Confederate Memorial on the State House grounds. Main Street is in the background. Courtesy of South Caroliniana Library

Mrs. Louise Owen LaRouche broke a champagne bottle on the City of Columbia, christening General Aero Company's first line from Miami to New York City. Courtesy of South Caroliniana Library

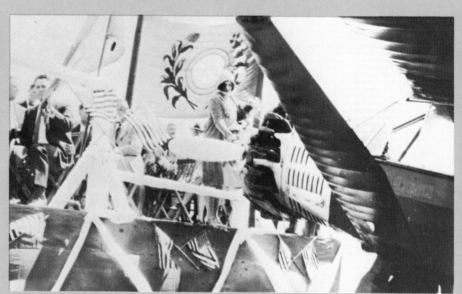

The E. W. Biggs family posed outside their home at 418 Brown Street in the late 1920s. From the Biggs family album in the South Caroliniana Library

The old covered bridge, which burned in 1925, crossed the Broad River between Camp Fornance and the St. Andrews area. Courtesy of Security Federal Savings and Loan Association

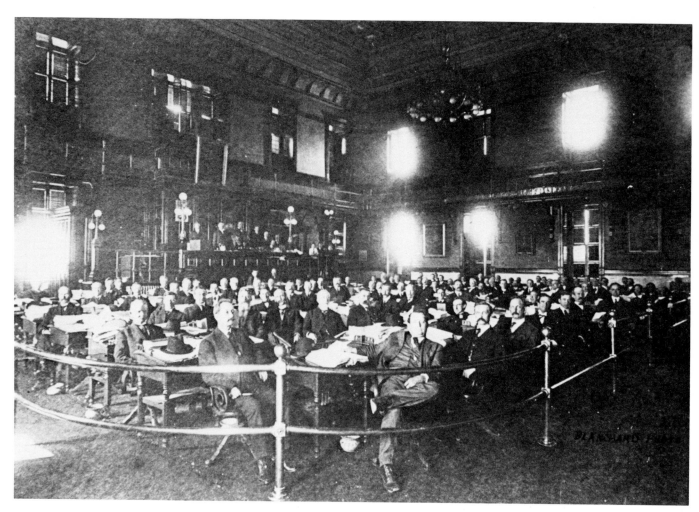

A photograph of the South Carolina Legislature in the early 1930s. Courtesy of
South Carolina House of Representatives

The Jefferson Hotel at Main and Laurel
streets offered baths in every room.
Courtesy of South Caroliniana Library

The ballroom of the Jefferson Hotel was the setting for elegant dinners and dances for several generations of Columbians. Courtesy of Dixie Electronics Inc.

Delta Air Lines flew the first air express out of Columbia's municipal airport, Owens Field, in 1936. Mayor L. B. Owens, for whom the field was named, right, watches the loading of the plane. Courtesy of the City of Columbia

Cast iron figures like this one, found throughout Columbia waiting to hold the reins of horses, were made by the thousands at the Palmetto Armory Iron Works. The public one, on a pole outside the armory, was taken down in 1924 when this photograph was shot. Courtesy of South Caroliniana Library

Central Chevrolet, still operating in Columbia today, was on the 1200 block of Hampton Street when this picture was taken in 1932. A Peter's Dry Cleaning delivery truck had parked in front of the car dealership. Courtesy of Security Federal Savings and Loan Association

The Seaboard Air Line trestle, running through Columbia along Lincoln Street from Pendleton Street to Olympia Avenue was built 1899-1900. Courtesy of Security Federal Savings and Loan Association

Owen and Paul Tailor Shop operated at this location on Washington Street for a number of years. Courtesy of South Caroliniana Library

University of South Carolina cheerleaders leading the crowd in a cheer in 1931. Courtesy of the University of South Carolina

Coeds at the University of South Carolina visiting in a dormitory room in 1930. The first dormitory for coeds opened in 1924. Courtesy of the University of South Carolina

A 1934 Fire Prevention Week parade being led by a uniformed police officer on a horse. Courtesy of South Caroliniana Library

The Tree of Life Synagogue, a reformed congregation, was organized in 1896. Courtesy of South Caroliniana Library

The original Market Restaurant, as photographed in 1935, grew to be one of Columbia's finest restaurants before closing in 1985. Owner Nick A. Papadea, far right on stool, is shown with his employees and a customer. Courtesy of Jim Papadea

The House of Peace Synagogue, an orthodox congregation, was built in 1935 and demolished in 1973. Courtesy of Columbia Newspapers Inc.

This scene of black housing in Columbia was taken in the 1930s. Courtesy of South Caroliniana Library

The interior of the Columbia Theater, located in the City Hall at Gervais and Main streets, was elegant. City Hall was built in 1900 and torn down in the mid-1930s to make way for the Wade Hampton Hotel. Courtesy of Historic Columbia Foundation

The Kinard house at 1400 Lady Street was one of the oldest houses in Columbia when it was torn down in 1945. This picture was taken when the house was for sale in the 1930s. Courtesy of South Caroliniana Library

The Lake Murray Dam, the nation's largest earthen dam when it was built, is northwest of Columbia. This construction photograph was taken May 15, 1929. Courtesy of South Carolina Electric & Gas Co.

A typical residence on the 900 block of Oak Street in the 1930s. Courtesy of South Caroliniana Library

Family photos of children in the 1930s and 1940s often included the nurse. Courtesy of Mrs. William N. Geiger

A shopper on Main Street in the 1930s was caught by a sidewalk photographer who then sold her the picture. Courtesy of Mrs. William N. Geiger

Columbians from all walks of life came to the Assembly Street market to buy fresh produce. Courtesy of South Caroliniana Library

A young girl shells beans while waiting to sell her produce at the market on Assembly Street. Courtesy of South Caroliniana Library

Golf tournaments attracted crowds at Forest Lake Club in the 1940s. Courtesy of South Caroliniana Library

A new shed stretched south down the center of Assembly Street in 1940. The shed was part of the federal Works Progress Administration. Courtesy of South Caroliniana Library

The main administration building at Allen University in the 1940s. Courtesy of South Caroliniana Library

University of South Carolina students gather in the basement canteen of Maxcy College in the 1940s. Courtesy of the University of South Carolina

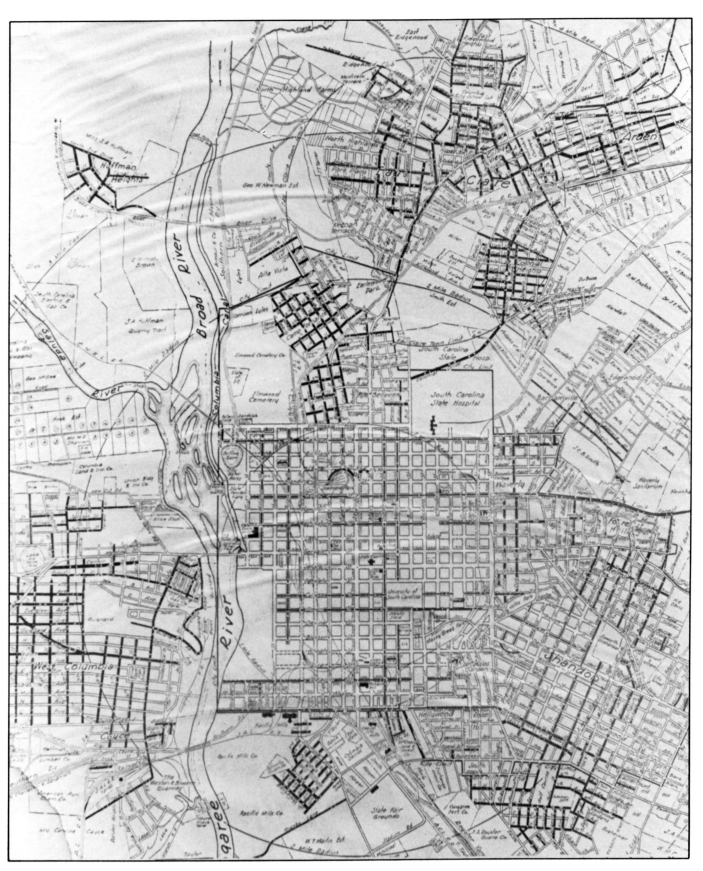

A 1940 map of Columbia showed the city's growth and pointed out that there were 239 streets with duplicate names. Courtesy of Columbia Newspapers Inc.

Soldiers caught buses to Fort Jackson at Main and Gervais streets during World War II. Courtesy of South Carolina Electric & Gas Co.

A Texaco service station was tucked behind the present South Carolina Supreme Court Building. Courtesy of South Carolina Electric & Gas Co.

The downtown showroom of Dixie Radio Supply in the 1930s. Courtesy of Dixie Electronics Inc.

The intersection of Main and Gervais streets at the Wade Hampton Hotel was busy in the 1940s. Courtesy of South Carolina Electric & Gas Co.

The Confederate Relic Room, inside the State House, was a monument to the Civil War and the Confederacy. The artifacts now are housed in the War Memorial Building. Courtesy of South Caroliniana Library

These seven Columbians—all daughters of Confederate soldiers—posed for a group photograph in the 1950s. Courtesy of Mrs. William N. Geiger

The Ridgewood Country Club, Columbia's first, was on the northern edge of the city at the end of the Eau Claire trolley line. It opened November 1, 1904, with only men allowed as members. It eventually opened its membership to women. Jack McGrail photograph, courtesy of South Caroliniana Library

This Delta flight was the first out of the Columbia Metropolitan Airport when it opened. The airport serves the area from Lexington County. Courtesy of the City of Columbia

In 1942, British Prime Minister Winston Churchill, third from left, visited Fort Jackson. Reviewing the troops with him were, from left, Gen. George C. Marshall, U.S. Army chief of staff; Field Marshall Sir John Dill of Great Britain; U.S. Secretary of War Henry L. Stimson; Fort Jackson commander Maj. Gen. Robert L. Eichelberger; and Gen. Sir Alan Brooke, chief of the imperial staff of Great Britain. Courtesy of the U.S. Army

The 2500 and 2600 blocks of North Main Street were residential areas in the 1940s. Courtesy of Mrs. William N. Geiger

Children enjoyed a University of South Carolina faculty picnic with their families at Sesquicentennial Park, developed as part of Columbia's 175th birthday celebration. Courtesy of Candy Waites

Outhouses were still a way of life for some residents of Columbia in 1952. Courtesy of South Caroliniana Library

Columbia Bible College students hung their laundry out in front of Ainsley Hall House in 1952. Courtesy of South Caroliniana Library

South Carolina Electric & Gas employees enjoyed E. F. Lever barbecue at a company picnic in 1950. Courtesy of South Carolina Electric & Gas Co.

137

The county treasurer, in his office at the Richland County Courthouse, which was later demolished, accepted $117,000 in county taxes from South Carolina Electric & Gas Co. in 1950. Courtesy of South Carolina Electric & Gas Co.

The city began addressing major drainage problems when seventy-two-inch storm drain lines were laid in the Rosewood Drive area in 1950. Courtesy of the City of Columbia

A city worker repairing a traffic light in 1951. Courtesy of the City of Columbia

University of South Carolina graduates walking in an academic processional across campus in 1950. Courtesy of the University of South Carolina

The Columbia Hotel is seen at left in this photograph looking east on Gervais Street from Sumter Street. Courtesy of the City of Columbia

The new South Carolina Farmers' Market off Bluff Road opened in 1952, featuring distribution warehouses and permanent sheds. Courtesy of the City of Columbia

Produce was sorted behind the booths at the Assembly Street Market in 1952, shortly before the market was moved to Bluff Road. Courtesy of the City of Columbia

The Columbia police headquarters and jail in 1952. Courtesy of the City of Columbia

The main squad room of the city police department had one small wooden desk and the traditional bulletin board of "wanted" posters. Courtesy of the City of Columbia

Columbia police officers showing off their new cars in 1952. Courtesy of the City of Columbia

The city jail in the 1950s was a series of small, individual pens. Courtesy of the City of Columbia

An exhibit by the City of Columbia in the mid-1950s, designed to show the city's growth. Courtesy of the City of Columbia

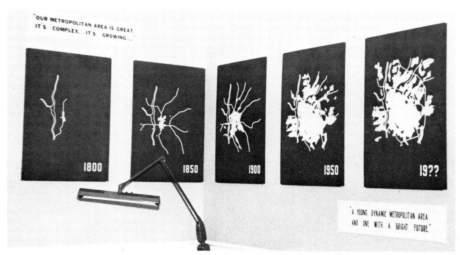

In 1955, the city fire department offered its old Mack hook-and-ladder truck for sale. *Courtesy of Columbia Newspapers Inc.*

Ladder trucks were used to replace bulbs in Columbia street lights in the 1950s. The old Eau Claire town hall is seen in the background. *Courtesy of the City of Columbia*

The Trinity Episcopal Church children's choir prepares for the Easter Day service in 1953. Courtesy of Candy Waites

A Columbian sits with her paintings at a Trinity Episcopal Church sidewalk art show in the early 1950s. Courtesy of Candy Waites

Main Street at midday in 1955 was buzzing with activity. Courtesy of Columbia Newspapers Inc.

Tanks rolling down Main Street during a parade in the mid-1950s. City Hall and the former Jefferson Hotel can be seen in the background. From the Dwight Cathcart collection, courtesy of South Caroliniana Library

Dr. Wil Lou Gray's pioneering Opportunity School offered adults a chance for added education in the 1950s. Courtesy of Columbia Newspapers Inc.

The South Carolina State Penitentiary, in 1955, had brick walls and wooden guardhouses. Courtesy of Columbia Newspapers Inc.

WIS television's tower dominated the downtown area in the 1950s. From the Dwight Cathcart collection, courtesy of South Caroliniana Library

Columbian Miriam Stevenson, Miss Universe 1955, rides in a parade through the city. From the Dwight Cathcart collection, courtesy of South Caroliniana Library

Crayton Junior High School being built in
the late 1950s on Clemson Avenue in
Forest Acres. The building was situated
next to Crayton Elementary School, thus
creating one of Columbia's first campuses.
The growth of the two schools paralleled
the growth of Forest Acres and the eastern
part of Columbia. From the Dwight
Cathcart collection, courtesy of South
Caroliniana Library

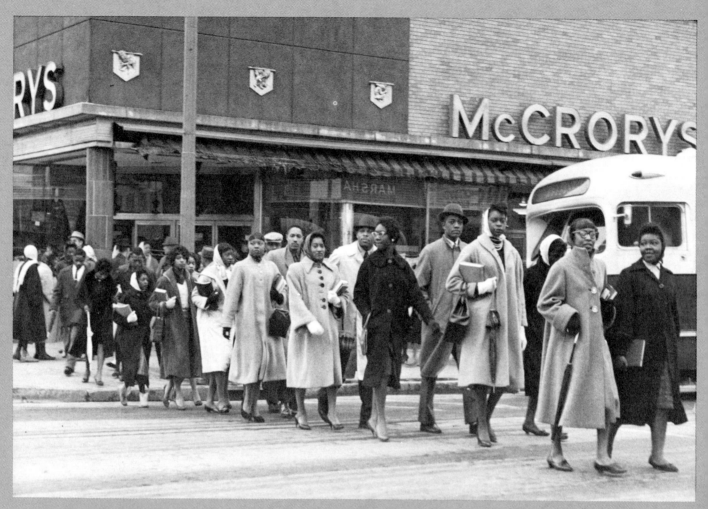

Columbia's only major racial
demonstration came in March 1960 when
blacks marched down Main Street.
Courtesy of Columbia Newspapers Inc.

Blacks, protesting racial discrimination,
sat at a lunch counter in Woolworth's on
Main Street in 1960. They were denied
service. Photograph by Victor Tutte

A bird's-eye view of Columbia in the early 1960s showed Longstreet Theater in the foreground. Skyscrapers included the new Federal Building, Cornell Arms, the Jefferson Hotel, the Wade Hampton Hotel, Number One Main Street, the Palmetto Building and the Barringer Building. Senate Street still ran along the south side of the Capitol. Courtesy of Columbia Newspapers Inc.

A winter 1961 snowstorm gave Columbians a rare opportunity to go sledding. Courtesy of the City of Columbia

Snowstorms are always a treat for Columbians of all ages. Photograph by Victor Tutte

Children enjoyed rides and birthday celebrations on the train that ran in Valley Park in the 1950s. Courtesy of Candy Waites

Columbia May Day celebrations attract ladies young and old to compete for queen and princess of May Day. Courtesy of the City of Columbia

A dedication evening was held in 1962 for the Kress Collection at the Columbia Museum of Arts. Cutting the ribbon are, from left, George Hartness, Mrs. Ruth Kress, Mrs. M. S. Whaley and Jack Morris. Courtesy of Columbia Newspapers Inc.

The Eau Claire High School football team enjoyed a pre-game dinner at the Shamrock Drive-In before their last game in 1961. Courtesy of Mrs. J. O. Butler

A city police officer directs traffic at Washington and Main streets. The Standard Federal Savings and Loan Association clock, later moved to a new location on Main Street, can be seen in the background. Courtesy of the City of Columbia

The Hotel Columbia, seen from Sumter Street, became a University of South Carolina dormitory before being demolished in 1972. The twenty-story NCNB Tower now occupies the site. Courtesy of Columbia Newspapers Inc.

The first blacks to enroll at the University of South Carolina since Reconstruction, from front, James L. Solomon, Henri Monteith, and Robert G. Anderson, signing forms and paying fees in the Naval ROTC armory as television cameras roll. Photograph by Victor Tutte

Horse races were held around the arena at the State Fair Grounds as late as the 1960s. Photograph by Victor Tutte

The Homecoming Court at Eau Claire High School in the early 1960s. Courtesy of Mrs. J. O. Butler

Columbia enjoyed a rare Christmas season snow in the early 1960s. Courtesy of Columbia Newspapers Inc.

*The Columbia skyline was growing
upward in 1961. The rock quarry near
Olympia is in the foreground. Photograph
by Victor Tutte*

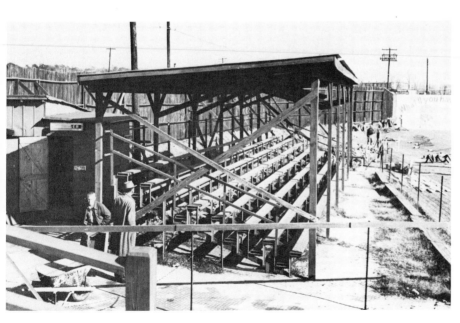

Some of Columbia's oldest black congregations still exist in the city's downtown area. The Arsenal Hill Club of Zion Baptist Church was photographed in 1961 when it reorganized. Courtesy of South Caroliniana Library

Renovation work is done on the Capital City Ball Park in the 1950s. Courtesy of the City of Columbia

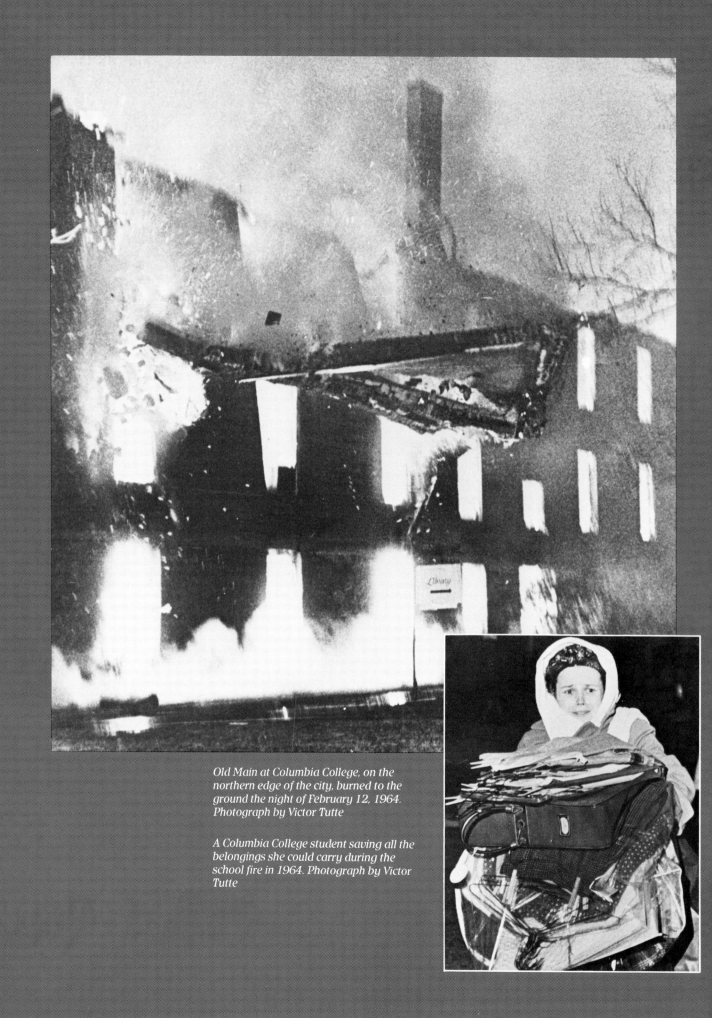

Old Main at Columbia College, on the northern edge of the city, burned to the ground the night of February 12, 1964. Photograph by Victor Tutte

A Columbia College student saving all the belongings she could carry during the school fire in 1964. Photograph by Victor Tutte

Fire Prevention Week in the 1960s meant parades and queens. Courtesy of the City of Columbia

The first floor of City Hall was remodeled during the 1960s. Courtesy of the City of Columbia

A veteran watches from the State House
steps as the Armed Forces Day Parade
moves down Main Street in the 1960s.
Photograph by Victor Tutte

A Seaboard Railroad conductor checks tickets on a midnight train out of Columbia in the 1960s. Photograph by Victor Tutte

Fort Jackson and City of Columbia officials met to sign papers in 1968, officially annexing the fort into the city limits. It is the only army base in the United States located within a city. Courtesy of the City of Columbia

White reaction to the civil rights movement of the early 1960s led to a brief resurgence of the Ku Klux Klan, shown here in a rally near Columbia. The organization today has fewer than 100 members statewide. Photograph by Victor Tutte

Saxon Homes, a public housing project, was built in the 1960s to provide housing for low-income citizens. Courtesy of the City of Columbia

City of Columbia officials inspecting substandard housing around the city during the 1960s. Courtesy of the City of Columbia

South Carolina's premier statesman, James Byrnes, and his wife greeting President and Mrs. Richard Nixon in 1969. The Nixons visited the Byrnes's Heathwood home. Courtesy of Columbia Newspapers Inc.

"South Carolina's capital city is looking toward its 200th birthday, still uncertain what it should celebrate. Some newcomers claim that Columbia lacks a special character or a central force that sets it apart. . . It is the geographic hub of the state where foothills meet plains. That location partly explains much of the city's history and its character. Quite a civic rainbow. A capital, a college town, a military city. . . Columbia's diversity should not be mistaken for lack of character. In that diversity lies its strength. . . . It is Everyman's city."

—Robert A. Pierce
"Columbia's Strength Lies in Her Diversity,"
The State (1985)

FIVE
TOWARD
CENTURY III
1970-1986

A s Columbia entered the decade of the 1960s, it reached a milestone. For the first time, its population exceeded 100,000, and also for the first time it was home to more non-native South Carolinians than natives.

The previous ten years had seen a spate of plans sponsored by various segments of the community. The most far-reaching had been the Doxiadis Plan adopted as the 1960s were coming to a close. The plan had been a community-wide effort, but it immediately ran into trouble. Perhaps it was the times. Perhaps Columbians had simply grown tired of planning. Or, maybe they most emphatically did not want their city to be "just like Toledo, Ohio." In a national article, an unnamed civic leader had singled out Toledo as a city worthy of emulation, but Columbia residents showed little enthusiasm. There were other events going on in the early 1970s that captured the local interest.

South Carolina celebrated its Tricentennial in 1970 with a state-wide observance that had decidedly mixed results. In the capital city, the Hampton-Preston Mansion on Blanding Street was purchased and restored, and two geometric domes were erected on either

side of it to serve as exhibition halls. There was a great deal of emphasis on the past—almost as if many wanted to forget the present, never mind the future.

The Tricentennial year was also the year that Columbia's public school system became a unitary one. Since the mid-1960s, a small number of blacks had attended previously all-white schools. Under the federally imposed unitary school plan, token desegregation was replaced by complete integration. Neighborhood schools became a thing of the past. Little consideration was given as to the social importance of schools being community centers to certain sections of the city such as Olympia.

The character of schools changed overnight. The most noticeable changes occurred in extracurricular activities. The city's coaches found their teams decimated by the wholesale loss of key players. During the 1960s, Eau Claire, Dreher, and Booker T. Washington high schools had won state championships. Before 1970, it was a signal honor to win a place among "The Marching 100" band of Booker T. Washington. After 1970, the school was lucky to have half that many in uniform. The changes

A typical summer haze softens Columbia's skyline. It is a sight familiar to the thousands of drivers who commute into the city on Interstate 126. Courtesy of Columbia Newspapers Inc.

elicited a great deal of public criticism.

Dissatisfaction led to a continual turnover of elected members of the school board. In fifteen years, the district had five superintendents. Despite the difficulties, parents, teachers, administrators, students, and public officials struggled to make the new system work. By the early 1980s, their efforts would appear to be paying dividends.

The city schools weren't the only ones with problems in the early 1970s. Students at the University of South Carolina, like others across the nation, rioted in May 1970. The Administration Building was ransacked, and the National Guard was called out to quell the disturbance. Scenes of the Guard, using tear gas to disperse rock-throwing student radicals on the tree-shaded campus, shocked Columbians.

The student riots, coming on the heels of an aggressive physical expansion of the University into nearby residential neighborhoods, created an antagonism that was similar to that of the antebellum years. The callous use of eminent domain to force long-time residents out of their homes left a bad feeling in a lot of Columbians.

By 1975, this unneighborly behavior had changed and working with nearby residents, the University began to make a strenuous effort to stabilize the residential neighborhoods adjoining the campus.

The expansion of the University was matched by the expansion of state government. Senate Street, behind the Capitol, was closed. New office buildings were built and the statuary on the State House grounds was rearranged. A multistory underground state parking garage led to a significant reduction in downtown parking woes.

Parking problems along Main Street had been increased, ironically, by the implementation of one recommendation of the Doxiadis Plan: the Main Street Mall. With brick paving, narrowed streets, new curbs, and plantings, automobile traffic was slowed. Five giant light poles—150 feet tall—marched down the center of the street, obscuring the historic vista of the State House from the old city limits at Elmwood. The lights became a target of abuse from many quarters and finally, early in 1986, were removed.

Although the Main Street Mall was adopted specifically from the Doxiadis Plan, much of the rest of the plan was ignored. Given the expansion that spread throughout the city between 1970 and 1986, however, Columbians did take the central theme of the plan to heart: "Recognition of the need for planning and the establishment of goals is the first step toward progress."

As the city's suburbs expanded into Lexington County, a new generation of Columbians began to take a second look at the older downtown neighborhoods—and they liked what they saw. The housing stock was solid and relatively inexpensive. There were neighborhood parks and tree-shaded streets. In the beginning, there were no formal plans, but once the process of neighborhood revitalization began, neighborhood

councils sprang up to keep a sharp eye on future development.

It was in Shandon, one of the city's 1920s suburbs, that the neighborhood revitalization began. Young couples moved in and within eight to ten years had transformed what was on the way to becoming a "transitional neighborhood" into a community attraction. The Shandon renaissance was cited by planners from all parts of the country. A byproduct of the Shandon story was the emergence of the so-called "Shandon Mafia," a group of concerned young men and women who have had a significant impact on the city's politics.

Others took note of what had happened in Shandon and soon the renovation process was repeated in the University East, Melrose Heights, Elmwood Park, and Cottontown neighborhoods. Connecting three inner-city residential neighborhoods was Five Points, a collection of small shops and stores. As the adjoining neighborhoods were rejuvenated, the nature of Five Points changed. Today, the older, more traditional businesses are outnumbered by restaurants, bars, and specialty shops. Five Points has become Columbia's place to dine and drink.

While the old southeastern portion of the central city was booming, revitalization in the area bounded by Main, Taylor, Harden, and Elmwood moved at a slower pace. There was little chance that the area would be saved by urban homesteading. Rather, adaptive reuse and rehabilitation of older homes and buildings for commercial use became the key to saving this once elegant residential neighborhood. Much credit for the transforming of this area from a slum into some of the city's most sought-after business space belongs to the Historic Columbia Foundation. Through persuasion, discussion and cooperation with the business community, the Foundation and its members worked to make the past a viable part of Columbia's future.

Among the many who listened and acted were city officials. A new historic preservation ordinance provided much-needed zoning regulations. On Main Street, the city took the lead in adaptive reuse by rehabilitating the Brown Building across from City Hall for use as municipal offices. That sent a message that Main Street was a respectable address again. The location of the new Richland County Judicial Center on the northern end of Main Street, and the building of the Palmetto Center midway between City Hall and the State House, created effective anchors around which subsequent development could cluster.

Surrounding the business district were institutions of higher education—all which expanded their physical plants in the 1970s. Columbia College rebounded from a disastrous fire that destroyed a portion of the campus. After experimenting briefly with co-education, the college settled back to being an all-female school. Benedict College achieved national recognition and financial support because of its innovative programs and new campus facilities. The University of South Carolina was expanding in all directions, but

*Students at the University of South
Carolina take to the streets in May 1970
to protest the Vietnam War. The National
Guard and Highway Patrol are attempting
to restore peace. Courtesy of Columbia
Newspapers Inc.*

took the time to restore the Horseshoe, the historic heart of the campus.

The impact of the University on Columbia was far greater than that of simply a larger student body and additional buildings. Culturally, it added new dimensions to the community. The first was in athletics with the great Gamecock basketball teams coached by the legendary Frank McGuire. The new Carolina Coliseum on Assembly Street provided an arena worthy of the Gamecock teams, and it gave the city a multi-purpose entertainment center. Once the Coliseum opened, Ringling Brothers Circus put Columbia back on its national tour.

From the academic side of campus, the University through its faculty and programs made tremendous advances. Under President James B. Holderman, the institution has attracted considerable notice in the area of international affairs: Columbians have had the opportunity to hear world leaders expound on a variety of issues. The school's accomplishments were no accident—they were the result of the "Carolina Plan," an academic blueprint for the University's development.

Planning was also apparent in the completion of the interstate highways that linked Columbia with most major eastern and midwestern markets. The opening of I-77 to Charlotte not only dramatically improved travel to North Carolina, it also led to new suburbs on the city's northeastern fringe. The I-77 area is now dotted with shopping malls, industrial and office parks and residential subdivisions. Still under construction is the southeastern

beltway which eventually will provide another bridge across the Congaree and link the northeastern suburbs with I-26 east to Charleston.

Commuting to work in Columbia has become a way of life for thousands of Midlands residents. Once sleepy country crossroads have become the capital's bedroom communities. There is no better example of this than the Irmo phenomenon. As late as 1961, "Irmore," as it was locally known, was the lowest town in the Lexington town pecking order, behind Gilbert and Pelion. Then came the development of several major industries followed by subdivisions. By the 1970s, Irmo was sprawling all over the sand hills and its high school was one of the largest in the state. Newer residents, knowing nothing of their town's past, boast that "Columbia is ten miles from Irmo."

While some residents of Columbia's suburban communities might say that they have nothing to do with the central city, hundreds of others have become the backbone of the volunteer groups that support the Columbia Music Festival, the Friends of the Richland County Public Library and other cultural groups. Like other new Columbians of earlier generations, they have come to the city because it was a good place to live—and they are willing to work to make it even better.

Established Columbia residents have welcomed the newcomers into their midst. A survey of the city's civic and cultural organizations reveals that almost all have been led in recent years by someone who moved to town within the past twenty years.

Substandard housing—for white families as well as black—was still a problem in Columbia in the 1970s. Courtesy of South Caroliniana Library

Housing along Lincoln Street in the 1970s was indicative of the poverty in the city. Courtesy of the City of Columbia

Growth and development, however, have brought some changes that have left voids in the city's cultural memory. With a multiplicity of high schools, old rivalries and attachments don't seem to mean as much as they once did. Columbia High has moved to the suburbs, and the old downtown building has been razed; Booker T. Washington High was closed, its students transferred to other schools, and the old classroom buildings demolished; Olympia High has become a middle school.

Gone along with the old high schools of the 1950s and 1960s are the student hangouts. Doug Broome's Drive-In on North Main was a landmark for white youngsters, while black teenagers frequented another Broome establishment, the Pig's Trail Inn.

The closing of Doug Broome's and the Market Restaurant, the moving of Cogburn's to Lexington County, the removal of head-in parking from Main Street, and the demolition of the city's grand old hotel, the Jefferson, were part of the price that Columbia paid for progress.

Even though it had seen better days, the Jefferson had continued to be the setting for the city's most important public and social functions. When the legislature was in session, it was generally acknowledged to be the "unofficial State House." When the walls of the Jefferson came tumbling down, the events that had been held there scattered to other facilities.

Some things change and, without question, Columbia has changed since World War II—but some things remain the same. The city's social season still is concentrated in a feverish five weeks between Thanksgiving and New Year's Day. Although the original reasons for the socializing no longer exist (the annual session of the General Assembly and Carolina's Commencement), no one has seen fit to alter the tradition of a hectic round of December party-giving.

Among the key ingredients of the social whirl are the debutante balls where young women officially are presented to society—generally during their sophomore years in college. The elegant Columbia Ball on Thanksgiving Eve formally opens the season. From that evening until the New Year is rung in, there are parties, dances, and balls galore. It is not unusual to find people attending three, four, or even more events in a single evening.

After a night on the town, breakfast at the Elite Epicurean or the Capital Cafe is a Columbia tradition. At opposite ends of Main Street, these two restaurants have welcomed a cross section of the city's population for years. Joining them on Main above the State House in 1986 is another Columbia gastronomical institution, the Dairy Bar, which was forced to move from its South Main location. There are hundreds of restaurants in the city (more than in tourist-catering Charleston) and each has its supporters, but none has woven itself into the fabric of local life as much as those on Main Street.

As South Carolina's capital city entered its Bicentennial year, it could look back with pride and see that it has managed to maintain a number of traditions and institutions that give it character. Along with tradition, however, has been a willingness to accept change. While during the 1960s and early 1970s, change was accepted grudgingly, it has been warmly embraced in the 1980s.

In 1978, when Kirkman Finlay Jr., was elected mayor, he focused his campaign on his vision for Columbia. It was a grand one, indeed: a revitalized downtown, the development of the river front, and a better quality of life for all Columbians. Not too many people thought that one man's vision would become reality, but after eight years even the doubters have become believers.

Since 1900, Columbians have cursed the numerous railroad tracks that lace the area between Assembly Street and the river. With the emergence of Lexington County towns as Columbia bedroom communities, the tracks and their often ill-timed trains became more than a mere inconvenience. Working together, the city, the railroads, and the business community sought and obtained federal funding to relocate the tracks so that a four-score-and-six-year problem soon will be no more.

Similarly, the building of the Palmetto Center office and hotel complex to anchor the midsection of Main Street was the result of cooperation between City Hall and the business community.

Working together—pulling together—for all Columbians has been one of the most important aspects of the city's recent history. There is no better illustration than the adoption of the present form of city government. Columbia still employs a city manager to handle the day-to-day operations, but the council is no longer elected by the voters at large.

Under the old at-large plan, no blacks had never been elected to council. Federal Court rulings upheld the plan's validity, but a number of Columbians believed it was wrong that some 40 percent of the population didn't have representation on the council. A new plan with four councilmen elected by district, two elected at large and the mayor elected at large was supported by the city's business, political, and civic leadership. After the plan was adopted by the voters in 1982, Luther J. Battiste III and E. W. Cromartie became the first elected black city officials in a century.

On its own, the city developed the Riverfront Park around the old waterworks and the Columbia Canal. This opening up of the city's long-neglected waterfront was an important component of the plans for the Congaree Vista. Unveiled in 1985, the plan, designed by South Carolinian Robert Marvin, outlines the ideal development of the land between Assembly Street and the river. Because of the relocation of the railroad tracks, there will be a lot of previously undeveloped land available. The Congaree Vista plan calls for five distinct corridors—residential, commercial, sales, light industrial, and green space—in order to attract residents back to the central city. The state's Vietnam memorial will be located in the Vista.

According to the 1980 census, for the first time in its history, the city proper has lost population, although the metropolitan area continues to grow. Columbia is still the largest city in the state, and the greater metropolitan area is among the fastest growing in the nation. Some elements of the Congaree Vista plans and related development activities already are beginning to take shape.

West of Assembly Street, across from the Carolina Coliseum will be the new $15 million Ira and Nancy Koger Center for the Performing Arts. In the 1930s, the Township Auditorium replaced the old Columbia Theater in City Hall in name only. For nearly a half century Columbians have yearned for an auditorium in which concerts and theatrical productions might properly be staged. Thanks to the cooperation of the University of South Carolina, private donors, and Richland County, at long last Columbia will get its performing arts center.

Like almost everything else about Columbia, the city's Bicentennial has been the result of careful planning. In 1978, several citizens met with Mayor Finlay to urge the city to think in terms of a five or six-year planning period. From these early meetings evolved the Columbia Bicentennial Committee, with civic leader O. Stanley Smith as chairman. Like its predecessor of a half century earlier, the committee planned a variety of events: neighborhood festivals, parades, pageants, fireworks, gala balls, an official history, and a movie. Committees were formed to involve as many citizens as possible. But this time, the planning for this civic birthday party included all segments of the community.

Columbia is still a mixture of old and new. Textile mills and cotton warehouses still operate in the city. Home-grown industries such as the Siebels Group and Colonial Life and Accident Company serve the nation. And foreign-owned companies dot the landscape.

How would those who have gone before have viewed Columbia of 1986? Thomas Taylor, George Washington, Wade Hampton III, and a host of others would no doubt be surprised at the transformation of a small southern country town into one of the fastest-growing metropolitan areas in the United States.

One Columbian of another generation who wouldn't have been surprised would be William E. Gonzales whose comments about the city in 1936 are just as appropriate today: "It is pleasant to think of Columbia as a place to which thousands have come to engage in life's strivings for advancement, and that those thousands now love this town as home, because those with whom they mingle are a kind and friendly people. Let us hope that, however greatly this rapidly growing city may expand, those qualities will never be lost."

Columbians of today and tomorrow might do well to keep in mind these words—not to enshrine the past, but to remember to incorporate the best of our city's heritage in planning for Columbia's third century.

A full moon rises high over a University of South Carolina football game in September 1978. Photograph by Victor Tutte

Children line up at a mailbox while Santa Claus mails their letters to the North Pole. Photograph by Victor Tutte

Columbians turning out on a rainy July 4, 1976, to celebrate their nation's Bicentennial. Photograph by Donald K. Woolley

The ruins of the old Cotton Mill on the west banks of the Saluda River still exist today, offering a picturesque setting across from the Riverbanks Zoo. From the Dwight Cathcart collection, courtesy of South Caroliniana Library

A typical Columbia ice storm in the late 1970s coating the city with an icy glaze and bending pine trees to the ground. The city suffered three major ice storms during the decade, all which caused some power outages lasting as long as a week. Photograph by Donald K. Woolley

Hundreds of farmers drove their tractors to Columbia and surrounded the State House in December 1977 to protest federal policies. Photograph by Victor Tutte

A 1978 labor union strike at the Olympia Mills in Columbia resulted in extensive damage to the mill's interior. The mills have been unionized since the 1930s. Courtesy of Columbia Newspapers Inc.

Columbia teens flocked to the Saluda River Rapids in 1978 to enjoy an escape from the heat. Courtesy of Columbia Newspapers Inc.

The Olympia Village area, surrounding the Olympia Mills on the south side of town, was still a quiet village in 1979. Courtesy of Columbia Newspapers Inc.

The UFO Coffee Club in the late 1960s and early 1970s was the center of Vietnam War protests until the city closed it. Courtesy of Columbia Newspapers Inc.

Main Street has taken on a new look with outside dining and high-rise hotels. Courtesy of Columbia Newspapers Inc.

Cloggers have been a regular feature in the modern annual Christmas parades. Courtesy of Columbia Newspapers Inc.

The congregation of the Forest Drive Baptist Church met at the Richland Mall Theaters in 1978 until their new church was built. Courtesy of Columbia Newspapers Inc.

The Arcade Mall, an inside shopping mall on Main Street, was bustling with activity in 1971. Courtesy of Columbia Newspapers Inc.

Columbians gathered on Main Street in 1977 to have a piece of cake and enjoy the Downtown Alive celebration. Courtesy of Columbia Newspapers Inc.

By the mid-1980s, the Wheeler Hill area had been transformed into one of the city's more prosperous communities. Courtesy of Columbia Newspapers Inc.

The Wheeler Hill neighborhood along Pickens Street was a poverty area in the 1970s. Courtesy of Columbia Newspapers Inc.

Gov. and Mrs. Dick Riley and Lt. Gov. and Mrs. Mike Daniel led the processional at the 1983 Governor's Inaugural Ball. Courtesy of Columbia Newspapers Inc.

The Little Red Schoolhouse was moved from the State Fair Grounds to Arsenal Hill Park in 1985. It is part of the city's continuing commitment to preserving its history. Courtesy of Columbia Newspapers Inc.

Columbians and their pets gathered on the lawn of Trinity Cathedral in October 1984 for the annual Blessing of the Animals by the Rev. Lloyd Edwards. Courtesy of Columbia Newspapers Inc.

The annual Trinity Bazaar attracted Columbians who wanted to purchase arts, crafts, and foods. The 1983 bazaar, in spite of the rainy weather, attracted its usually large crowd. Courtesy of Columbia Newspapers Inc.

University of South Carolina president James B. Holderman received a duplicate of the Heisman trophy from football star George Rogers in 1980. Courtesy of the University of South Carolina

Columbia's sportsmen find some of the best fishing in the area in the three rivers along the edge of the city. Courtesy of Columbia Newspapers Inc.

The Rev. I. DeQuincey Newman, right, took
the oath of office October 4, 1984. The
long-time Columbia resident was the first
black elected to the state Senate since
Reconstruction. Courtesy of Columbia
Newspapers Inc.

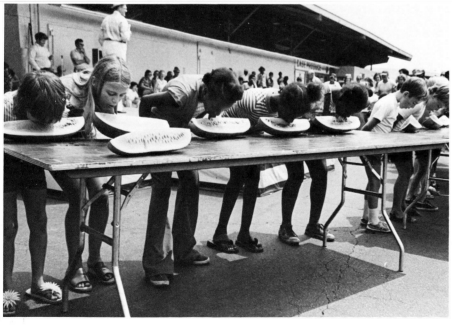

Annual festivals at the State Farmers'
Market off Bluff Road attract thousands
of residents who want to buy produce and
participate in games such as the water-
melon eating contest. Photograph by
Donald K. Woolley

The Governor's Annual Carolighting Ceremony attracts thousands of residents each year. The program of songs and music is capped by the lighting of the state's Christmas tree. Courtesy of Columbia Newspapers Inc.

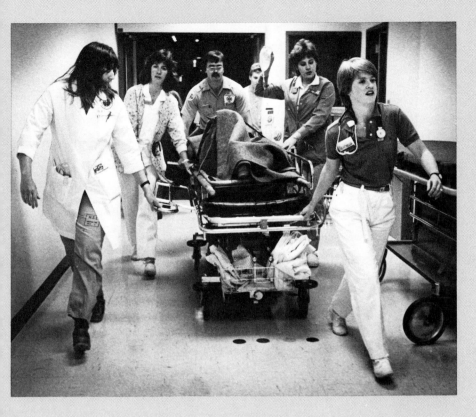

The staff at Richland Memorial Hospital, a regional trauma center, going through a training exercise. Courtesy of Columbia Newspapers Inc.

Warehouses in the Columbia area were used to store cotton until the 1970s, although cotton had ceased to be the state's major crop. Courtesy of the University of South Carolina

Cranes lifting Columbia's new 150-foot-tall lights in place on Main Street in 1977, starting nine years of controversy. Courtesy of Columbia Newspapers Inc.

In 1986, Columbia's controversial Main Street lights come down, once again clearing the view down Main Street to the State Capitol. Courtesy of Columbia Newspapers Inc.

A view of Main Street, looking north from the State House. The city's controversial street lights stand tall, blocking the view down the center of the street. Photograph by Victor Tutte

Fort Jackson, the nation's largest U.S. Army basic training post, had both male and female soldiers by 1980. Courtesy of Columbia Newspapers Inc.

A 1979 snowstorm drives most Columbians indoors as city officials try to clear the streets. Courtesy of Columbia Newspapers Inc.

The circus comes to town each spring, and local officials and celebrities are tapped to ride the elephants from the train station to the Carolina Coliseum. Traffic waits as the elephants parade by. Photograph by Donald K. Woolley

The Riverfront Park was opened by the city in 1984. The restored Columbia Canal area offers walking paths along the river and an area for outdoor concerts. Courtesy of Columbia Newspapers Inc.

The mayor and four new city council members—including the first blacks elected to the council since Reconstruction—take the oath of office in 1983. Mayor Kirkman Finlay Jr., center, is joined by council members, from left, Luther J. Battiste III, Paul Z. Bennett, Rudolph C. Barnes, Jr., and E. W. Cromartie II and their wives. Councilmen William C. Outz, left rear, and T. Patton Adams look on. The oath is being administered by the late Judge Lincoln Jenkins. Courtesy of Columbia Newspapers Inc.

The Benedict College choir prepares for the re-dedication ceremonies of Antisdel Chapel on campus. More than $115,000 was spent renovating the 1923 chapel in the heart of the campus. Courtesy of Columbia Newspapers Inc.

Columbians flock to Lake Murray for recreation. In this scene from the late 1970s, swimmers dive off the concrete dam. Photograph by Donald K. Woolley

*Western rodeos come to the State Fair
Grounds annually, giving local residents a
front-row look at a cowboy sport.
Photograph by Edward L. Kalsch*

The Palm Terrace restaurant in the Columbia Marriott opened in 1983. The atrium hotel was a first for the city. Courtesy of Columbia Newspapers Inc.

The grand opening gala of the Columbia Marriott and twenty-story Palmetto Center on Main Street marks the beginning of the revitalization of downtown in 1983. Courtesy of Columbia Newspapers Inc.

Students participating in the University of South Carolina's annual Homecoming Fair paddle canoes in the reflection pond of the Thomas Cooper Library. Courtesy of the University of South Carolina

South Carolina's political parties come to Columbia every two years to elect officers and conduct business at their state conventions. The 1986 convention of the South Carolina Democratic Party was held in Township Auditorium. Courtesy of Columbia Newspapers Inc.

Prisoners stroll through the interior of Cellblock One at the State Penitentiary.
Photograph by Jack Hillwig

A prisoner at the State Penitentiary plays basketball on an outside court.
Photograph by Jack Hillwig

197

Columbians turned out in the early morning hours on Sunday, July 21, 1985, to watch the Wade Hampton Hotel imploded. It was demolished to make way for the twenty-five story AT&T building. Courtesy of Columbia Newspapers Inc.

A 1986 view of Main Street from the State Capitol shows the Wade Hampton Hotel and the five tall lights gone. Courtesy of Columbia Newspapers Inc.

On March 22, 1986, Columbians spent the
day celebrating their city's Bicentennial.
That evening, they danced the night away
at three Bicentennial balls. Courtesy of
Columbia Newspapers Inc.

A bird's-eye-view of downtown Columbia in 1986 shows the State House grounds and office complex, the start of construction of the AT&T building, and a growing downtown area. Courtesy of Columbia Newspapers Inc.

NOTES ON SOURCES

In writing the text for *Columbia: Portrait of a Capital City*, the authors used published and unpublished reference materials in the South Caroliniana Library. There are, quite literally, hundreds of manuscript collections that deal with life in Columbia. Similarly, the library has assembled a sizable collection of books, articles, and newspapers. The library's card catalogue and printed manuscripts guide list the specific references to Columbia and Columbians.

For anyone who wants to read about Columbia in greater detail, the sesquicentennial history *Columbia: Capital City of South Carolina, 1786-1936* and the South Caroliniana Society's *A Columbia Reader* are readily available in the city's bookstores and libraries.

In addition to the materials used for the text, the Caroliniana's rich photographic collections provided a large percentage of the illustrations appearing in this book.

INDEX

Walter Bellingrath Edgar, professor of history and director of the Institute for Southern Studies at the University of South Carolina, is the author and editor of numerous books and articles on South Carolina and South Carolinians. His most recent work is *History of Santee Cooper, 1934-1984*. Professor Edgar has been an active member of the Columbia community, serving as president of the Historic Columbia Foundation, the Friends of the Richland County Public Library, the Columbia Kiwanis Club, and the South Caroliniana Society. He, his wife Betty, and their daughters, Eliza and Amelia, attend Trinity Episcopal Cathedral.

Deborah Kohler Woolley, manager of Public Information for the South Carolina State Development Board, has made Columbia her home since graduating from the University of Tennessee's College of Communications. She was a staff member of the *State* and business editor of the *Columbia Record*. She holds a master of arts degree from the University of South Carolina and is the author of several magazine articles on Columbia. She is active in the Columbia community, serving on the boards of the Better Business Bureau and the Columbia Action Council.